1993

This book provides a concise, illustrated history of Great Britain over the past three centuries, from its formation as a sovereign state in the Union of England and Scotland in 1707 to its partial loss of sovereignty in the accession to the European Community which was finally confirmed by the result of the referendum of 1975.

The general theme of the volume is the interaction of state and society. Specifically this involves the interplay of parliament and the electorate. The long-delayed introduction of democracy is seen as a consequence of the inherent conservatism of British – or at least of English – society. Reactionary causes were more powerful, and the forces of inertia more durable, than radical campaigns – a conclusion perhaps reinforced by the results of the 1992 election.

CAMBRIDGE CONCISE HISTORIES

A Concise History of Britain

CAMBRIDGE CONCISE HISTORIES

This is a new series of illustrated 'concise histories' of selected individual countries, intended both as university and college textbooks and as general historical introductions for general readers, travellers and members of the business community.

Titles in the series:

A Concise History of Germany
MARY FULBROOK

A Concise History of Greece
RICHARD CLOGG

A Concise History of France
ROGER PRICE

A Concise History of Britain: 1707–1975
W. A. SPECK

A Concise History
of Britain
1707–1975

W. A. SPECK

Professor of Modern History, University of Leeds

CAMBRIDGE
UNIVERSITY PRESS

Published by the Press Syndicate of the University of Cambridge
The Pitt Building, Trumpington Street, Cambridge CB2 1RP
40 West 20th Street, New York, NY 10011–4211, USA
10 Stamford Road, Oakleigh, Melbourne 3166, Australia

First published 1993

Printed in Great Britain at the University Press, Cambridge

A catalogue record for this book is available from the British Library

Library of Congress cataloguing in publication data
Speck, W. A. (William Arthur), 1938–
A concise history of Britain, 1707–1975 / W. A. Speck.
p.   cm. – (Cambridge concise histories)
Includes bibliographical references.
ISBN 0 521 36400 0. – ISBN 0 521 36702 6 (pbk.)
1. Great Britain–History.   I. Title.   II. Series.
DA470.S74   1993
941–dc20   92–20187   CIP

ISBN 0 521 36400 0 hardback
ISBN 0 521 36702 6 paperback

For my brother
Jack

CONTENTS

ILLUSTRATIONS

PREFACE

Any historian who attempts to write an overview of British history from the Anglo-Scottish Union of 1707 to the entry into the European Community is bound to be heavily indebted to the work of others. In such a small compass their contributions will inevitably be compressed to the point of distortion, and I apologise here to the many scholars whose writings I have synthesised so succinctly that they might not even recognise them or, if they did, would disown them. This book is not intended for them. Rather it aims at readers who, while they might be on nodding terms with the outlines of modern British history, seek a concise résumé of recent scholarship.

Since my own area of expertise is the eighteenth century, two colleagues at Leeds, David Steele and Richard Whiting, kindly read the chapters on the nineteenth and twentieth centuries. They, together with the anonymous referees for Cambridge University Press, offered criticisms which saved me from many blunders. Any which survive are entirely my responsibility.

I wish also to thank others who helped to make this book possible. Leeds University granted me a term's study leave in the spring of 1989 which enabled me to make a start. Adrian Wilson rented me his house in Cambridge at intervals where much of the research was undertaken. My brother Jack generously let me have the use of his flat in Filey where most of the writing was completed. Mary Geiter and my daughter Jackie read rough drafts and suggested appropriate improvements. Finally William Davies of Cambridge University Press was very supportive throughout.

NIAS, Wassenaar   December, 1992

Introduction

This concise history covers the period from the formation of the United Kingdom of Great Britain in 1707 to the entry of the British into the European Economic Community in the 1970s. Thus the chronology spans the whole history of Britain in the precise sense that the Union of 1707 brought it into being, ending the separate sovereignty of England and Scotland, and was for the Scots at least the 'end of an auld song'; while membership of the EEC was a partial surrender of British sovereignty, even if few were prepared to recognise it or admit it.

To cover such a long period in such a short compass is inevitably to reduce a symphony to a sleeve note. Some concentration is required to pick out the main themes. The principal theme is that change has been evolutionary rather than revolutionary. The peaceful adjustment of institutions and social structure to changing circumstances has been largely due to the fact that, since the Glorious Revolution of 1688, machinery has always existed for effecting such changes without resort to rebellion or revolution. There have not been wanting rebels or revolutionaries – Jacobites in the eighteenth century, Jacobins in the early nineteenth, for example – but they have never appealed to more than a minority. The majority have either acquiesced in the status quo or accepted that desired changes could be obtained by persuasion rather than by force. The ruling class was always susceptible to being persuaded because it remained answerable to the electorate through parliament, which never ceased to function as a representative institution even in the so-called 'age of oligarchy' in the middle of the eighteenth century.

1   The Great Seal of Great Britain after the Union, 1707

Another cause of the peaceful transition of British society from an oligarchy to a democracy has been that, for most of the time, the economy literally delivered the goods. Alternatives to the existing system only became widely attractive in rare intervals when such buoyancy was not sustained. By and large people were not only spared starvation but, through an unprecedented growth of population, the standard of living was at worst sustained and at best improved. This was not regarded as a mere coincidence. On the contrary, the connexion between limited or mixed monarchy and economic growth by contrast with absolutism and stagnation or decline was hammered home in learned treatises and crude propaganda.

Clearly the themes of consensus politics and population expansion underpinned by economic development do not hold for Ireland. The tragic history of 'John Bull's other island' is not incorporated except when it could not be ignored by people on the mainland.

Chronologically the book has been carved up conventionally into centuries. It has become fashionable of late to talk about a long eighteenth century starting before 1700 and stretching to 1832. But the

Unions with Scotland at the beginning and Ireland at the end give the short century more coherence. The Union of 1707 altered the constitutional framework and the very nature of the British state. It brought Great Britain into being. Similarly the Union with Ireland set a new agenda for British politicians. Each century has a short analytical introduction followed by chapters narrating those political events which illustrate the main themes. The narrative tries to avoid being a mere chronicle. As far as possible the emphasis remains on the interaction between state and society as epitomised in the fluctuating relationship between parliament and the classes who controlled it and the electorate to whom they had ultimately to answer.

1

Eighteenth-century Britain

It has been claimed that the single most important event in Britain's history occurred millions of years ago, or whenever it was during the formation of the earth's surface that the English Channel and North Sea were formed, separating the British Isles from the continent of Europe. Certainly the fact that the mainland of Great Britain, comprising England, Scotland and Wales, is an island has been of central importance to its development as a nation. Thus the isolation of the British made their history, in some respects at least, different from the rest of Europe's.

One of the crucial differences was the county. Until the Local Government Act of 1972, which became effective in 1974, England and Wales were divided into fifty-two counties and Scotland into thirty-three. In the eighteenth century the English counties were administrative units. Each had a sheriff, a commission of the peace, and a militia presided over by a lord lieutenant. The post of sheriff was irksome and expensive, and men tried to avoid selection for it. By contrast the offices of justice of the peace and deputy lieutenant of the militia, though they were unpaid, were coveted since they bestowed status on their incumbents. The justices administered a great deal of statute law, either singly, in pairs, or collectively, at the sessions held every three months and therefore called quarter sessions. They would refer the most serious cases, involving capital crimes, to the assizes, generally held twice a year in the county town, when a judge from one of the common law courts at Westminster would preside over the trials.

1	Dumbarton
1a	to Dumbarton
2	Stirling
3	Clackmanan
4	Kinross
5	Renfrew
6	Bute
7	Arran
8	West Lothian
9	Mid Lothian
10	East Lothian
11	Peebles
12	Selkirk
13	Lanark
14	Westmorland
15	Flint
16	Rutland
17	Huntingdon
18	Bedford
19	Middlesex

Map 1   County map of Great Britain

The county was not just a unit of administration but served as a focus for local loyalties. At one time it might even have superseded loyalty to the nation, at least among the upper sections of society who have been referred to as 'the county community'. By 1707, however, allegiance to the nation had largely overcome such localism. Nevertheless the notion that men were Cornishmen or Yorkshiremen as well as Englishmen is of vital importance in the history of England, even if their identities as denizens of Denbighshire or Midlothian were not quite as crucial to Welshmen or Scots.

For England had been divided into thirty-nine counties since before the Norman Conquest. The boundaries of some, especially in the peripheries, such as Kent and Northumberland, reflected the borders of ancient kingdoms, while others, particularly those in the Midlands, had the appearance of specific creation. The Principality of Wales had contained counties since the Middle Ages, when the shires of Anglesey, Caernarvon, Merioneth, Carmarthen, Cardigan and Flint had been established. The March, too, contained a couple of medieval counties, Glamorgan and Pembroke. But it was dominated by the Marcher lordships which were semi-autonomous bailiwicks. It was to bring order into this lawless region that an act was passed in 1536 'to turn the whole of Wales into shires'. Then the counties of Brecknock, Denbigh, Monmouth, Montgomery and Radnor were substituted for Marcher lordships, and other lordships were absorbed into the existing shires. Wales was consequently assimilated into England. Each county was supplied with a sheriff, justices of the peace, and members of parliament, two for Monmouthshire, one for each of the other twelve. Scotland's thirty-three counties varied considerably in size. The largest, Ayr, Argyll, Inverness and Sutherland, compared with the larger English shires. The smallest were smaller than Rutland. Daniel Defoe referred to 'the little shire of Renfrew, or rather a barony, or a sheriffdom, call it what you will'. And Renfrewshire was far from being the smallest. Yet they all returned members to the British parliament after 1707: twenty-seven at every election; six at alternate elections. Thus Bute was linked with Caithness, Clackmannon with Kinross, and Nairn with Cromarty in order to ensure thirty representatives from Scottish counties in accordance with the conditions made for the representation of the northern kingdom under the Union.

Elections revealed in a dramatic way where power lay in the shires of eighteenth-century Britain. The leaders of county society, the peers and principal gentry, would meet at the assizes or the quarter sessions or some specially convened assembly to try to agree on candidates to be knights of the shire in the forthcoming parliament. If they could reach agreement then no contest would occur. It was almost unknown for the forty-shilling freeholders who formed the bulk of any county's electorate to set up a rival to the nominees of the leading magnates of the shire. Rutland, the smallest English county, had only a handful of resident peers and gentry. The Earl of Nottingham, with his country house at Burley on the Hill, was the most substantial magnate of the shire in the early eighteenth century. Below him such country gentlemen as the Halfords and the Sherards also wielded influence. These three families virtually monopolised the county's representation. In Northamptonshire some nine families disputed the distribution of the county's seats between them; the Berties, Cartwrights, Cecils, Dudleys, Finches, Hattons, Ishams, Montagus and Spencers. Yorkshire, the largest county, was far too big to be dominated by a few aristocrats and gentry. At the outset of the eighteenth century such grandees as the dukes of Devonshire and Bolton, the earls of Burlington, Carlisle, Strafford and Wharton, along with half a dozen lesser lords and innumerable gentry, exerted substantial electoral interest. Peers of the realm tended to be thinner on the ground in Wales. Glamorganshire was dominated by about twenty-five gentry families, chief of which was the Mansell family, with houses at Margam and Briton Ferry. Where the Mansells had been prominent in county affairs for generations, the middle of the seventeenth century had witnessed the arrival of some newcomers to the elite, including Philip Jones, a military adventurer during the Civil Wars, who established a dynasty which was to represent Glamorganshire in parliament. In Scotland a ruling elite was even more firmly entrenched. Argyllshire, for example, was controlled by the Campbells, dukes of Argyll, who nominated members of their family to the county seat. The main cause for this control over Scottish counties was that many of them were quite small while the number of voters in them was tiny in comparison with those of England and Wales. Where Yorkshire mustered over 15,000 voters and even Rutland had over 500, the largest number of voters in a Scottish county was in Peeblesshire, which had about 100. As in England and Wales the franchise was based on the ownership of

freehold property worth forty shillings a year, which was valued at
£400 Scots in 1681. But unlike the situation south of the border the
freehold had to be land held of the crown. This, more than low land
values in the northern kingdom, restricted county electorates there.

The hegemony of the great landlords in the counties was upheld in
a variety of ways. For one thing they were wealthy, and wealth and
power are not unusual combinations. But wealth alone did not usually
make landlords powerful. When City businessmen tried to acquire
seats in parliament by scattering guineas among electors in constituencies where they were strangers it provoked disapproval and was
counter-productive. Contemporaries expected candidates to have what
they termed a 'natural' interest in a locality, by which they meant long-
term residence and, in counties, the ownership of substantial acres.
Even new entrants into the ranks of rural magnates by no means
acquired electoral interests overnight. It took time, sometimes a
generation or two, for a gentry family to acquire a 'natural interest' in
county affairs.

The wealth of such families was based on their landed estates.
Typically they owned a country house. These could range in size and
prestige from the palaces of the dukes of Devonshire and Marlborough
at Chatsworth and Woodstock to modest manor houses. The owners
of such properties generally leased farms to tenants from whom they
received rents. These tenant farmers, though they were in an
economically subordinate relationship to their landlords, were not
necessarily dependent upon them socially. Landlords needed tenants as
much as tenants needed farms, if not more so. When profits from
selling surplus farm produce fell to levels which made the payment of
wages to labourers and rents to landowners problematical, then farms
lost their appeal to tenants. This situation occurred frequently in the
rural economy; in the early 1700s through poor harvests, and between
1730 and 1750 through over-abundant harvests which lowered the
price of agricultural produce. In both periods landlords found
themselves having to write off rent arrears and to leave farms
untenanted. Even the purely business relationship, therefore, was one
of give and take based on a mutuality of interests.

But the relationship of landlords and tenants went much further than
the cash nexus. They both formed part of a traditional society which,
while it expected due deference from inferiors to superiors, also placed

patriarchal obligations on the elite. Entertainment at the country house, participation in village sports like cricket and foxhunting, even joint worship at the parish church, helped to cement the local community. Of course this patriarchal ideal was breached. Some landlords rackrented tenants and ended leases if rents were unpaid. The game laws confined the destruction of game to the proprietors of land worth £100 a year, and farmers who defied them could be prosecuted for killing hares, partridges and pheasants even on the fields they farmed. Landlords absent in London or elsewhere were not available to entertain their neighbours or join them in prayer. Yet although such types were the butt of satire the deference communities of rural Britain were not for the most part based on fear and hatred so much as on a respect for mutual obligations.

The realities of rural relationships were tested whenever the efforts of the landed elite to control the outcome of county elections broke down and rival candidates emerged to compete for the votes of the forty-shilling freeholders. Since there was no secret ballot until 1872 the votes of many county electors are known through the survival of poll books which record how they were cast. One of the most striking features of any county poll book is the propensity of parishes to vote *en bloc* for the same candidates. There can be no doubt that this was due to the fact that neighbours of a territorial magnate polled for those whom he backed. Some would be his tenants, since, although freehold tenure normally meant owner occupation of land, leases for lives counted for electoral purposes as freeholds. It could have been, therefore, that some landlords dragooned such tenants to the polls under threat of not renewing their leases when they expired. But the electoral behaviour of only a small minority can be satisfactorily explained in terms of such coercion. The canvassing of votes by landlords and election agents was undertaken in terms which left no doubt that their disposal was regarded as a favour and not as a formality. The majority of freeholders followed the lead of the substantial landlords in their midst through an acknowledgment that they had a natural right to expect such recognition of their role in the county rather than through fear of reprisals.

A significant proportion of the county electorates blatantly disregarded the wishes of their social superiors and polled contrary to them. The parish clergy in particular exercised an independent role in county elections and often persuaded their parishioners to poll in a body with them. This was because the bulk of the inferior clergy were Tories in the reign of Queen Anne. Not for nothing was the Tory party then often dubbed 'the church party'. Where the leading landowners were Whigs their wishes would be defied by the Anglican ministers and many of their congregations.

A contested county election soon revealed the limits of deference. As long as they could avoid a contest, however, the landed elite invariably kept control of the representation of the shires. During the height of the 'rage of party' when the landed elite was bitterly divided between Tories and Whigs it often proved impossible for the county magnates to reach agreement. Between 1701 and 1734 there were ten general elections at each of which on average nearly half the English counties were contested. At the following six general elections the proportion dropped to less than a sixth. The last great county contest between Tory and Whig candidates in the eighteenth century is generally agreed to have been that fought in Oxfordshire in 1754. That was by then quite unusual, most county elites having come to terms, agreeing to share the representation and thereby to avoid contests.

The landed elite also controlled the outcome of many borough elections. Where there were only 122 county seats in the parliament of Great Britain there were 436 borough seats. This imbalance might seem to have given townsmen overwhelming importance in national affairs. Yet in fact most boroughs returned country gentlemen to parliament in the eighteenth century. Where in any House of Commons there might be about fifty lawyers and as many merchants, along with perhaps 100 army and navy officers and civil servants, even these also owned land, while the majority of MPs were mere landowners. This was the case even before the Property Qualifications Act of 1711 obliged members to possess real estate to the value of £600 in counties and £300 in boroughs. Deference explains the hold of the landed elite over many boroughs as well as over the counties. The relationship between the owners of country houses and the burgesses of towns in their neighbourhood gave rise to the same mutual obligations as that which cemented the relations of landowners and tenants on a landed estate. For country houses were far more than machines for their owners to live in. They were also symbols of the wealth and status of their occupants. Such houses provided employment for builders, carpenters, glaziers, painters, stonemasons and other craftsmen concerned with their fabric; for cabinetmakers, clockmakers, cutlers, drapers, pewterers, potters and silversmiths to furnish them; for brewers, butchers, grocers, hatters, hosiers, tailors, vintners and other tradesmen to supply apparel and provender; and for butlers, chambermaids, coachmen, cooks, gardeners, valets and other domestics to minister to them. Thus a large country house on the outskirts of a parliamentary borough, a not unusual situation, could be the biggest consumer of goods and services and employer of labour in the neighbourhood. It would be a rash or very independent tradesman who would vote against the wishes of the owners of such houses as Berry Pomeroy, home of the Seymours just outside Totnes in Devon, or Dunster Castle near Minehead, owned by the Banks family, or Studley Royal, a stone's throw from Ripon, occupied by the Aislabies. It was part of the natural order of things that Totnes should be a pocket borough of the Seymours, Minehead of the Banks's and Ripon of the Aislabies.

Similarly in Scotland the Ayr boroughs returned the nominees of the dukes of Argyll and earls of Bute. Scottish borough representation was confined to fifteen seats, which were distributed among sixty-seven burghs, all except Edinburgh being grouped into fourteen combinations of four or five, which presided in rotation at successive general elections. Like the Scottish counties they had small electorates which were very susceptible to the influence of local landed magnates. Where the freeholders in the counties were called barons, and were men of sufficient substance to be above barefaced bribery, the voters in some burghs, the Perth and Stirling groups for instance, were among the most venal and corrupt in Britain.

In England the franchises in some boroughs helped local landlords to get a grip on their representation. This was particularly true in the case of those where the right to vote was vested in properties known as burgages. Peers and gentry made a point of purchasing burgages in order to control a majority of voters. Thus the Duke of Newcastle acquired ownership of those in Aldborough and Boroughbridge in Yorkshire, and with them the nomination of the four members who sat for those boroughs. Even where the franchise was vested in civic office, such as aldermen, councillors or freemen, gifts to the corporations, like the Earl of Bridgwater's provision of a new town hall at Brackley, could secure a controlling interest. Where the electorate was enfranchised through residence rather than real estate or office, for instance in boroughs where householders voted, then entertainment and 'treating' went a long way towards securing one.

More important than the franchise in creating opportunities for the local landowners to exert a dominant influence in a borough, however, was the number of voters. The electorates of all those boroughs which returned candidates recommended by a landed patron tended to be small, Stamford in Lincolnshire with some 500 voters being the largest under the complete sway of a single landlord, the Cecils of Burghley House. While substantial landowners could sit for towns with over 1,000 voters, this was by no means due to patronage alone. The dukes of Bedford had extensive property in Westminster, and many tradesmen who were dependent upon their custom polled for their candidates in contested elections there. But these were a tiny minority of the total electorate of at least 6,000. Such large constituencies were beyond being manipulated by patronage or bribery.

As in the counties the incidence of contests declined in the boroughs in the first half of the eighteenth century. Again the turning point came with the general election of 1734. In that year 113 of the 269 English and Welsh constituencies went to the polls. At the following election, held in 1741, only 76 polled; and at the next, in 1747, a mere 55.

The main reason for this fall in the boroughs was that a struggle between two rival interests had been resolved in favour of one of them. During the reign of Queen Anne many boroughs witnessed struggles for control between Tory and Whig magnates. Thus Bury St Edmunds saw bitter rivalry for one of its seats between the Tory Davers family and the Whig Herveys. The government could tip the balance between such rival interests, ensuring a Whig victory when it inclined in favour of that party and a Tory success when it leaned towards the Tories. Under Anne the government gave its support to the Tory party at some elections and to the Whigs at others. Under the Hanoverians, however, only Whigs were so favoured. The result was that many Tories gave up the unequal struggle, especially when the outcome of the 1734 election revealed that the ministry could retain a majority even when the counties and large boroughs returned opposition candidates.

The electoral system, however, never entirely atrophied even in the central decades of the century. There was a core of constituencies, consisting mainly of boroughs with large electorates, which were regularly contested and offset the oligarchic tendencies of the age. As the century progressed and these urban centres grew, a distinctly bourgeois element emerged in British society which could make its voice heard in politics.

The emergence of the English middle class has been located in London between 1680 and 1730. Certainly the capital was the only town capable of sustaining a recognisable bourgeoisie in the late seventeenth century. At that time it had about 500,000 inhabitants, over 8 per cent of the total population of Britain. No other city numbered its inhabitants in six figures or even high five-figure sums. Bristol and Norwich could boast about 30,000 each, while another five had over 10,000. So London was a giant, dwarfing every other town in the kingdom. The people who went there not merely replenished a population which would otherwise have dwindled due to a high death rate but actually increased it. It has been estimated that something like one in six of the British population must have gone there for some part of their lives in the century before 1750.

Although London continued to grow in the eighteenth century it did not do so at the same rate as the overall population, which expanded from about 7 million to 11 million. By 1800 therefore the capital contained a smaller proportion of the total than it had done in 1700. Meanwhile the number of towns with 10,000 or more inhabitants approximately doubled, while others grew towards that size. It is arguable what constituted the minimum population for a community to be described as a town. Contemporaries were clearly prepared to consider to be such what would be regarded as villages today. Urban historians seem to have settled on a population of 2,500 as the appropriate measure for urbanisation. In 1700 about one in six of the population lived in towns of that size or over, while by 1800 the ratio had changed to one in three.

Urban growth took place in various communities. Some were leisure towns like Bath, the Las Vegas of eighteenth-century Britain, and Brighton, its Atlantic City. Many older county towns like Shrewsbury and York became centres for the local gentry who stimulated luxury trades and devoted themselves to assemblies and horse-racing. Elsewhere urbanisation was associated with manufacturing areas such as the metalworking district of the midlands, the textile towns of Lancashire and Yorkshire and the ports of Bristol, Glasgow and Liverpool.

These urban centres developed a distinctly bourgeois life-style. They catered not only for businessmen but for a burgeoning professional class. While entrepreneurs could realise fortunes or bankruptcy, opportunities for clergymen, doctors and lawyers led to the expansion of these professions in the eighteenth century.

Business enterprise was stimulated in the first half of the eighteenth century by growing demand from both the domestic and overseas markets. As the increased productivity of the agricultural sector of the economy led to a fall in food prices, so surplus income was generated, especially among town dwellers who benefited from cheaper foodstuffs by being able to afford manufactured products. Thus demand increased for metal utensils and pottery, for example, stimulating production of the products of Birmingham, Sheffield and Staffordshire. At the same time the expansion of the North American colonies, and the policy of prohibiting manufacturing there so as to benefit domestic production led to the export of these commodities across the Atlantic. Such developments stimulated growth not only in manufacturing towns but in ports such as Bristol, Liverpool and Glasgow which served the American markets. Not that all businessmen who sought to satisfy these demands prospered. There were business failures as well as successes to record in the eighteenth century, and these increased towards the end as population expansion began to force food prices upwards while overseas trade was disrupted by the War of American Independence and the wars against revolutionary France more than it had been by previous hostilities. Yet on the whole the challenges of meeting consumer demand caused the businessmen of the ports and manufacturing towns of eighteenth-century Britain to increase rather than to lose wealth. This increased prosperity among the business community showed itself above all in the physical development of towns. The workshops and warehouses of the manufacturers and merchants were prominent features of the urban landscape.

The growth of the professions also had an impact on the physical appearance of towns. While it was not a great period for church building some provision was made by Anglicans for the growing towns. A grandiose plan to build fifty new churches in London alone had to be cut down to size, though at least a dozen were constructed in the capital. Elsewhere difficulties in providing new buildings were overcome, as the survival of several in manufacturing districts, such as the exquisite church at Bierley near Bradford, testifies. On the whole, however, the dissenters made more impact on towns than did the established church. Dissent indeed became largely an urban phenomenon during the course of the eighteenth century, at least until Methodists seceded from the Church of England after Wesley's death. Before that Presbyterians, Congregationalists, Baptists and Quakers formed conspicuous congregations to rival those of the established church. Their chapels and meeting houses became prominent features of townscapes. Despite the Corporation Act of 1661, which restricted civic office to communicating Anglicans, the Presbyterians at least played a leading part in public affairs. Their ministers, who numbered about 1,400, were generally regarded as dignitaries on a par with the established clergy.

The legal profession also burgeoned in the eighteenth century. Lawyers prospered in an age where the law was increasingly resorted to, especially after an act of 1731 insisted that legal proceedings should be conducted in English. The services of barristers were required in the London law courts and in assize towns in the provinces. Daniel Defoe found Preston 'full of attorneys, proctors and notaries'. Attornies acted not only as the arbitrators of all manner of disputes, but also served to legalise the complex transactions of a commercial society. Thus they acted as counsel for a litigious aristocracy and gentry, drew up their wills and negotiated their property deals and marriage settlements. Some became land stewards and even estate agents. Besides such time-honoured roles as clients of the landed elite there were new opportunities for lawyers. For example, they drew up the private bills which required enactment to facilitate enclosure agreements, the establishment of turnpike trusts, schemes to make rivers navigable and ultimately to construct canals. Such measures involved them not only with landowners but also with the business interests of market towns, ports and manufacturing centres. Attornies thus shared in the opportunities afforded by urban growth in the period, and their houses graced the more affluent parts of the Hanoverian townscape, such as the High Street in Burford and the 'Ivy' in Chippenham.

Doctors' houses too were among the more conspicuous of those of the so-called 'pseudo-gentry' of the towns. Indeed their incomes probably aroused more comment and envy than those of any other profession. The clergy, after all, were on the whole not among the more affluent citizens in towns, while many country curates scraped a living on £50 a year or less. Lawyers' fees invited criticism, but recourse to the law was not strictly necessary and affected only a minority. Sickness, however, struck every family in the land from the highest to the lowest. Recourse to a 'doctor', therefore, was essential, whether it involved calling in a physician for the upper classes and substantial bourgeoisie, an apothecary for the lower middle class, or a 'wise man' for the labouring poor. Theoretically there was a legal distinction between physicians and apothecaries which the College of Physicians tried to sustain. In practice, however, it proved impossible, and the growing demand for medicinal skills led to them being alike referred to as doctors during the course of the eighteenth century. Top physicians could command fees which gave them incomes of £5,000 per annum, as much as a country gentleman of substance. Even apothecaries earned enough for Adam Smith to comment that their 'profit is become a by-word, denoting something uncommonly extravagant'. Eighteenth-century medicine witnessed no great advances, though the increasing use of opium relieved pain and the introduction of inoculation did much to eliminate smallpox. Hospitals were founded in London and twelve provincial cities in the reigns of George I and George II. These were the prime centres for advances in surgery during the period. Given the almost complete ignorance of the causes of infection, however, dirty instruments probably ensured that more patients were sentenced to death from septicaemia by the surgeons than were saved by their skills.

Where most hospitals were founded through private charity, the state maintained Chelsea and Greenwich for wounded and veteran soldiers and sailors. Both had been established before the eighteenth century, but were substantially extended under the early Hanoverians to cope with the extra pressures brought to bear upon them by the expansion of the armed forces and their involvement in major wars. The growth of the military establishment increased the numbers of permanent army and navy officers who swelled the ranks of the professional classes. It also brought into existence what has been termed a 'military-fiscal state' to provide the sinews of war. A bureaucratic apparatus was created in the admiralty, the board of trade, the ordnance, the treasury and the navy office, staffed by clerks who formed an embryo civil service. The revenue departments for the collection of customs, excise and stamp duties also employed an increasing number of officers. By the middle of the eighteenth century what would nowadays be considered to be the civil service probably numbered about 16,000 men.

The growth of an urban middle class led to the development of a bourgeois culture. One manifestation of this was the newspaper and periodical press. This began in London, which had its first daily paper on sale in 1702. By the middle of the century there were over a dozen papers, appearing daily, bi-weekly or tri-weekly. Meanwhile a provincial press had made its appearance, with around forty papers published in various towns, some of them boasting two while a few, like Newcastle upon Tyne, had three. Where in 1700 the total weekly sales of newspapers had been less than 50,000, by 1760 it was over 200,000. The newspapers were supplemented by periodicals of which the most successful was the *Gentleman's Magazine* which began publication in 1731. Significantly it was originally subtitled the *Trader's Monthly Intelligencer*. The press created a network of communication which was skilfully exploited by the radical politician John Wilkes in the publicity campaign he mounted for his cause.

By the accession of George III, therefore, there were two political structures in Britain. One was the restricted society of aristocratic connections, based for the most part on electoral interests in small boroughs. The other was the middle classes of the expanding towns and cities which were responsive to political appeals such as that orchestrated by Wilkes.

It would be a mistake, however, to assume that what has been called an 'alternative structure of politics' was automatically radical in its views. On the contrary, the British middle classes showed themselves to be steadfast in their support of the constitution. If they could be persuaded that it was under threat from above, as many were during the Wilkes campaign and the early stages of the resistance of the American colonies, then they were prepared to adopt a radical stance. But if they were convinced that it was threatened from below, by American rebels after 1775, by Catholics in 1780, by radical politicians in 1784, and by 'Jacobins' in the 1790s, then they were even more ready to take up a reactionary posture. Above all when it was actually threatened by rebellious, Catholic, Jacobin Irishmen in 1798 then they rallied to the defence of the constitution in church and state.

2

From the Anglo-Scottish Union to the Union with Ireland

The Union of England with Scotland in 1707 which brought Great Britain into constitutional existence was more of a shotgun marriage than the consummation of a long-standing love affair. On the eve of the Act as it was called in the southern kingdom, or Treaty as it was known in the northern, relations between the two were in fact deteriorating. Although both rejected James VII and II in 1689, and accepted William and Mary, the consequences of the Glorious Revolution caused friction between them. The main problem as far as most Scots were concerned was that they were caught up in the wars against France to which William committed his new realms. Scotland became one of the cockpits of conflict, for the Stuarts retained much more active support there than they could command in England. The Jacobites, as the supporters of the exiled James and his son James Edward were known, defeated Williamite troops at the battle of Killiecrankie in August 1689, but their leader, James Graham of Claverhouse, died in the action. Though government forces won at Dunkeld later the same year, their victory only obtained a sullen and uneasy peace in Scotland. The massacre of the Macdonalds at Glencoe for tardiness in taking the oaths of allegiance was intended to teach Scots inclined to follow them in their defiance that the government would not tolerate even token resistance.

A more material disaster due to involvement with England was the Darien scheme. Scottish merchants were frustrated in their search for overseas markets by being excluded from English colonial trade. Thus at a time when extra-European commerce was stimulating what has

2   Queen Anne receiving the Treaty of Union between England
and Scotland, 1706

been termed the 'commercial revolution', Scots were prohibited from
trading with England's colonies. They therefore attempted to establish
a Scottish colony on the isthmus of Panama, and in 1698 founded the
fort of New Edinburgh there. This thorn in the side of Spain did not
suit William's diplomacy, and he ordered English colonists and
merchants to boycott it. The Darien colony never prospered, and after
being threatened by a Spanish expedition was abandoned in 1700.

The frustration of many sections of Scottish society found expression
in the last parliament to meet in Edinburgh. After its election in 1703
various measures were passed to focus resentment against England.
The most serious of these was the Security Act, so called because it
required securities for Scottish trade and the Presbyterian Church to be
given by England. Unless these were forthcoming the Edinburgh
parliament would declare a successor to the throne of Scotland other
than the head of the House of Hanover whom the English parliament
had chosen to succeed Queen Anne. This was a potential declaration of

independence, undoing the union of the crowns which had been achieved under the Stuarts. Although the Act required that successor to be a Protestant, it was clear to contemporaries that it partially unlocked the door to the return of the Pretender, as James Edward, by then the Stuart claimant, was called, even though like his father he remained a Catholic. The English parliament retaliated with an act requiring Scotland to settle the succession there by the end of 1705 or risk economic sanctions.

Out of this impasse, which at one time looked like ending in open war, emerged the Union. As well as threatening the Scots the English parliament offered to appoint commissioners to negotiate with the Scottish estates. Politicians in Edinburgh also drew back from the brink, whether through fear of hostilities or inducements from the English treasury. At all events two sets of commissioners duly convened in London. Negotiations for a Union had reached a similar stage in the 1690s only to founder. On this occasion, however, terms were thrashed out with remarkably little trouble.

The most immediately pressing conditions were that England and Scotland should merge in the United Kingdom of Great Britain, and that the succession to the British throne in the House of Hanover should be upheld. These not only took the heat out of the immediate crisis but in the long run proved to be the most enduring.

A principal inducement to persuade the Scottish commission and the Edinburgh parliament to accept the Union was Scotland's admission into the English economy on advantageous terms. Thus Scots were allowed full access to England's markets, including its colonies, while some Scottish industries, notably coal and salt, were protected from English competition.

Arrangements were also made to compensate Scotland financially for costs incurred by the Union. The Scottish tax base was much smaller than that of England, and her share of British taxation had to be nicely calculated. The relative yields from the excise, for example, were fixed at a ratio of 1:36. It was also agreed to phase it in gradually rather than impose it immediately. Thus malt was not to be brought into line with the English malt tax until after the end of the war with France. Scotland's national debt was minuscule in comparison with England's, so before she bore the full brunt of the burden an 'equivalent' of just under £400,000 was paid to compensate for it. This sum, which was paid to the creditors of the Darien company and others who had suffered from English measures, undoubtedly sweetened the pill of the Union north of the border.

To some modern observers the arrangements made for representing 'North Britain', as it was officially to be called, in the British parliament made the Union a particularly bitter pill for the Scots to swallow. Certainly the number of seats allotted to Scotland, forty-five, seems meagre since the county of Cornwall alone sent forty-four MPs to Westminster. Had there been a system of representation based on individuals then Scotland, with about a million inhabitants, should have obtained some 100 seats to offset the 513 for the 5 million or so people in England and Wales. Contemporaries, however, did not base the criteria of representation on individuals. There was no serious consideration given at the time to the notion that the number of representatives should be related to the total population. In the absence of a census until 1801 the figure could only be guessed anyway, and although there were some intelligent guesses, particularly about the size of the English population, there were some pretty wild ones too. Insofar as there was any notion of the number of seats being related to some kind of objective criteria it was to the proportion of taxation which particular regions contributed. There were complaints, for instance, that the relatively lightly taxed south-western counties of England were over-represented compared with the more heavily taxed 'home' counties. On this basis Scotland did not do too badly out of the Union, for its contribution to the British treasury was significantly less than the ratio 45:513, as we have seen in the case of the excise. On that ratio Scotland would have obtained only twenty-eight seats in the British parliament.

The terms agreed by the commissioners had to be ratified by the two parliaments. To get the Treaty through the Edinburgh parliament presented difficulties. There it had only to pass one House, since the Scottish estates met in a single chamber; but that House was deeply divided against itself. There was a strong Jacobite party of so-called 'Cavaliers' who were intent on exploiting the succession issue to secure the restoration of the direct Stuart line. Then there was a 'Country' party, staunchly Presbyterian and anti-Jacobite but so resentful of England's treatment of Scotland since the Revolution that they were prepared to keep the succession question open until satisfaction had been received from the southern kingdom. Together these were strong enough to outvote the 'Court' party which took its orders from Whitehall. They were reinforced by public opinion wherever it could make itself felt. For the Union was hotly debated in Scotland, and its opponents were more vociferous than its supporters. Advocates of the Treaty tried to sell it as the only way to avoid economic disaster. In some respects their arguments were not unlike those in favour of the Treaty of Rome at the time that Britain was debating joining the European Economic Community. To carry on as an independent entity would be ruinous. To join England in full partnership would produce an economic miracle. Opponents of the Treaty asserted that Scotland could survive economically. But their main objections were political. The loss of sovereignty and of nationhood after centuries of independence would be a catastrophe for Scotland.

Despite massive disapproval of the Treaty outside parliament it accepted the terms. This was due to the defection from the opposition of a group known as the 'flying squadron' which attached itself to the Court and carried the Union against Cavalier and Country intransigence. Much has been made of the motives of this group. To some historians they were statesmen who had a long-term vision of their country's future. On the other hand the inducements held out by the English government to them have led one historian to describe the Union as 'probably the greatest "political job" of the eighteenth century'. Certainly some of the squadron received substantial sums from the £20,000 paid out from England during the negotiations. As one of the ministers involved was to put it: 'We bought them.'

Having passed the Scottish parliament the Union ran into no serious difficulties in Westminster. This was partly due to the fact that the prevailing majority in both Houses was of Whigs, a party devoted to the Revolution settlement and the Protestant succession in the House of Hanover. They saw an incorporating union as the best guarantee of their endurance. The Tories raised some objections, mainly to the impact that the incorporation of a predominantly Presbyterian country would have on Anglicanism in the new nation. They prided themselves on being the party of the Church of England and ensured that its establishment was guaranteed in the final Act. This offset an act for the security of the Scottish church which the Edinburgh parliament had insisted upon as an essential pre-condition of accepting the Treaty.

In the years immediately following its ratification Scottish critics of the Union had the cold comfort of being able to claim 'We told you so.' For there was no economic miracle after 1 May 1707, when the kingdom of Great Britain came into being. Indeed the introduction of new taxes added extra burdens to Scotland's economy. The malt tax, an excise on a major product, was particularly resented since it was introduced a full year before the end of the War of the Spanish Succession in breach of the agreement that its introduction should be delayed until hostilities ceased. Other developments were also held to be infringements of the spirit if not of the letter of the Union. The abolition of the separate Scottish privy council and the extension of the harsher English treason laws to Scotland were resented. In 1712 the guarantees to the Presbyterian Church were jeopardised by the passing of the Patronage Act. Perhaps above all the honour and dignity of the Scottish peerage was impugned. By a curious clause of the Treaty peers in Scotland were not allowed to sit by hereditary right in the House of Lords but elected sixteen of their number to represent them there. When the Duke of Hamilton was elevated to an English duchy he was not permitted to enter the upper House, and yet was denied the right to vote for the sixteen representative peers.

This accumulation of dissatisfaction culminated in a resolution being moved by a Scottish peer in 1713 which aimed at the dissolution of the Union. It was defeated by a mere four votes.

After the accession of the House of Hanover the frustrations felt by many Scots were exploited by Jacobites in the rebellion of 1715. The Pretender had actually tried to exploit them as early as 1708 in an abortive expedition to the Firth of Forth. Now his supporters led by the Earl of Mar raised his standard again. If Mar had been a better leader his declared aim of restoring the independence of Scotland might have been achieved. Instead he dithered, giving the Duke of Argyll time to organise resistance. Even so the Jacobite forces outnumbered Argyll's by over two to one at the battle of Sheriffmuir. Though both sides claimed victory neither really won. Nevertheless Mar's withdrawal from the field marked the end of the rebellion.

The 'Fifteen saw fighting in England too. Indeed it was the most serious challenge which the English Jacobites posed to the Hanoverian regime. It is true that only a handful took up arms on behalf of the

3   King George I

Pretender; but they had the sympathy if not the support of many Tories who felt alienated from the new dynasty.

The party with a natural majority in England and Wales was feeling the full brunt of proscription. Having won six out of seven general elections before 1715 they were defeated at the polls in that year, beaten, they were convinced, by the fact that the crown gave its backing to their opponents. Certainly there was little love lost between George

I and the Tory government which held power in the last four years of Anne's reign. Its withdrawal from the War of the Spanish Succession and negotiation of the Treaty of Utrecht were regarded as betrayals of their allies, of whom the Elector of Hanover was one. George was also convinced that the Whigs were four square behind his claim to the throne, whereas many Tories were Jacobites. The flight of two Tory leaders, Viscount Bolingbroke and the Duke of Ormonde, to the Pretender's court in France seemed to confirm these suspicions. It also helped in the prosecution of the former prime minister, Robert Harley, Earl of Oxford, and in the elimination of Tories from top to bottom of the administration. So purges took place from the privy council to the commissions of the peace. This led a majority of Tories to withdraw their allegiance from George I, even if few declared it for 'James III'. Those that did rise up in the north-east of England got as far south as Preston in Lancashire before being defeated by government forces.

The defeat of the rebellion left the Whigs a clear field to perpetuate their own power and they took full advantage of it. In 1716 they passed the Septennial Act extending the statutory interval between elections from three to seven years. This was done deliberately to prevent government from being accountable to the electorate, which had consistently shown a preference for the Tories. Whig appeals to the people became less and less compelling as the party lost election after election. They won a clear majority at only one of the five general elections held in Anne's reign. Although they emerged victorious from the polls in 1715 they were right to apprehend that another contest in 1718 might well reverse that result. Not only did the electors show a marked preference for Tory candidates in parliamentary elections, they tended to do so in local elections too. Thus the City of London ceased to be the Whig power base it had been under Charles II and instead elections for common councillors went increasingly in favour of Tories during the reigns of William and Anne. This trend was confirmed after the accession of George I. So solid was the Tory grip on the City that in 1722 no Whig stood as a parliamentary candidate there. In an attempt to assert control over London's municipal affairs the Whigs passed the City Elections Act in 1725 which gave the Whig-dominated Court of Aldermen a veto over the predominantly Tory common council.

This evasion of the electorate was an admission that the Whig

4   Sir Robert Walpole in the House of Commons

party's supremacy was not based on popular support. On the contrary, its hold on power, so complete that Britain in the early eighteenth century has been described as a one-party state, was established by the elimination or suppression of alternatives. The Tory party was proscribed and an early appeal to the electorate was thwarted. Any challenge to the regime from the lower orders was checked by draconian legislation. A series of acts passed in George I's reign demonstrated that, however much the Whigs might have appealed to

'Liberty and Property' during the Revolution, they came to uphold property rather more than liberty after the accession of the House of Hanover. The Riot Act of 1715 made it a capital offence for twelve people or more to remain assembled when ordered to disperse by a justice of the peace. It also prescribed the death penalty for violent attacks on buildings. The Waltham Black Act of 1723, inspired by the depredations of deer stealers, made some fifty capital offences, including appearing in disguise on the highway.

In view of such repressive measures it is hard to accept the notion that Walpole presided over a period of political stability resting on a consensus. And yet Sir Robert's ministry was an interlude of relative stability following the upheavals of the seventeenth century and before the rise of radicalism in the later eighteenth. Moreover there was a consensus in the sense that the majority, in England at least, accepted the Revolution settlement and the Protestant succession. Most Tories even seem to have rejected the divine, indefeasible hereditary right of kings and to have accepted the sovereignty of the crown in parliament and its right to change the succession. Some Tories, even some of the populace, turned to Jacobitism as an alternative to the regime. How many will never be satisfactorily ascertained, and will therefore always arouse controversy. The degree of commitment to Jacobitism has indeed become the Loch Ness monster of eighteenth-century history. The true believers are convinced not only that it existed but that it was huge. They relate the equivalent of alleged sightings, out-of-focus photographs and sonic soundings. The sceptics remain unconvinced. But outside Scotland active support for the Pretender was meagre, as those who were prepared to rise on his behalf in 1715 and 1745 bitterly acknowledged. As for other alternatives, such as republicanism, outside a small coterie of intellectuals there is scarcely a trace.

Not that political discourse was totally subdued in these decades. Religion continued to fuel controversy and to provide bones of contention between Tories and Whigs. Tories championed the Church of England against its rivals. Where under the later Stuarts the main threat to the Anglican establishment had seemed to come from Roman Catholicism, after the Revolution dissent appeared more formidable. The Toleration Act of 1689, permitting the separate worship of Protestant dissenters, was followed by the founding of Presbyterian, Independent, Baptist and Quaker congregations in many communities.

5 'George's Combat'. Engraving showing the battle between King George II and Jacobitism, 1745

It left on the statute book, however, the Test and Corporation Acts by which only communicating Anglicans were supposed to hold offices under the crown or in corporations. Many Presbyterians breached this monopoly by taking communion in the established church to qualify themselves. These occasional conformists, as they were known, became a major party issue under Queen Anne. An Occasional Conformity Act was passed by the Tories in 1711, penalising the practice. It was, however, repealed by the Whigs in 1718, and thereafter frequent indemnity acts were passed to protect dissenters from prosecution for breaking the Test and Corporation Acts. But a campaign to repeal the acts in 1736 was resisted by the Whig government. It was mounted by dissident Whigs who had gone into opposition to Walpole. The fact that they were so sympathetic to dissent made it difficult for them to join with Tories in an opposition or 'Country' party against the Court.

There were several attempts during Walpole's long ministry, which lasted from 1720 to 1742, to effect a combination of his opponents to try to bring him down. The chief issue upon which both Tories and opposition Whigs could unite was the alleged corruption of his administration. Charges that Walpole was corrupt were raised at the outset when he was accused of covering up fraudulent dealings in South Sea stock. In 1720 the South Sea Company had undertaken to convert the unfunded national debt, amounting to some £31,000,000, into its own stock. Since the government did not stipulate that the conversion should be at par the company stood to gain if the market value of the stock rose above par. The greater the difference between the two values the more the company profited. Every means at its disposal were therefore used to force up the price of its stock, including the bribing of courtiers and ministers. The artificially inflated market peaked with £100 of stock selling for £1,000. Then the crash came, and many were ruined in the South Sea Bubble. Scapegoats were sought, first among the company's directors, then in the cabinet and even at court. Some sacrifices were thrown to the wolves, the chancellor of the exchequer being expelled from the House of Commons and sent to the Tower. But Walpole, whose own hands were clean, protected his colleagues from further investigations. For his pains he earned the nickname of 'screen master general'. Had the Tories got their act together for the 1722 general election they might have made significant gains by capitalising upon the Bubble. But in the event their organisation was feeble. Although more contests occurred than at any other election in the eighteenth century, many were fought not between Tories and Whigs but between rival Whig candidates.

During the ensuing parliament some dissident Whigs went into opposition to the Walpole ministry and tried to ally with the Tories. The main achievement of this Country coalition was the defeat of the excise scheme in 1733. This was a measure proposed by Walpole to counter the smuggling of tobacco and wine which cheated the treasury of unpaid customs duties. Goods would be imported into bonded warehouses and excises paid on their withdrawal for sale in Britain. To police this system would require an expansion of the numbers of excisemen with powers of search, which its opponents characterised as an extension of executive tyranny. Petitions poured in objecting to the proposal. Walpole's majority slumped in parliament to the point where he felt it prudent to abandon the idea.

The opposition tried to clinch its success in the general election of 1734. Although 'Country' candidates fared well in the larger constituencies, where Court supporters who dared stand were mostly defeated, the ministry nevertheless emerged from the polls with a parliamentary majority. In terms of votes cast Walpole undoubtedly lost this election. But he survived because he retained the support of members returned from the smaller boroughs, most of whom did not even face contests from rival candidates. The opposition complained that they had been robbed, and that Walpole owed his survival to corruption. But that was far too crude an explanation of the Court's control of the electoral system. Prior to the Septennial Act of 1716 many small boroughs had witnessed contests between rival Whig and Tory candidates. What had clinched the outcome in them had been the backing given by the Court to one side or the other. During Anne's reign that support had alternated between the parties. In 1702, 1710 and 1713 the Court had leaned towards the Tories; in 1708 towards the Whigs. After Anne's death the full weight of government patronage was given to Whig candidates in the general elections of 1715, 1722, 1727 and 1734. The result was that by the fourth consecutive electoral contest many Tories simply gave up the unequal struggle, leaving their rivals a clear field. As long as the Court could count on the Whigs, therefore, it had a built-in majority.

And yet Whig support could not be taken for granted. After the excise crisis a substantial group of 'patriot' Whigs went into opposition. More serious for Walpole was his alienation of the Prince of Wales and the Duke of Argyll, for they were the keys to electoral success in two crucial arenas, Cornwall and Scotland.

Frederick, eldest son of George II and Queen Caroline, had a stormy relationship with his parents. In 1737 he quarrelled with them, and went into opposition to Walpole. At the general election of 1741 his considerable electoral interest in Cornish constituencies, which had previously been placed at the disposal of Court candidates, was used to oppose them.

Court patronage was usually sufficient to ensure that the majority of the forty-five Scottish MPs supported the government of the day. Indeed the subservience of the Scots at Westminster became a commonplace of Country propaganda. Since most of the issues dealt with in the parliament of Great Britain primarily affected England there were few occasions for the forty-five to do other than to go along with the government. When issues affecting Scotland cropped up, however, it was another matter. One such surfaced in 1736 with the Porteous riots. Captain Porteous had become a hated figure in Scotland for ordering troops to fire into a crowd attending an execution, killing six of them. Although sentenced to death for murder he was granted a reprieve, upon which some 4,000 people broke into the gaol where he was imprisoned and lynched him. Unable to apprehend the culprits the government used parliament to impose a punitive fine on the city of Edinburgh. Scottish MPs and peers protested that this punished the innocent rather than the guilty. Amongst those most angered by the measure was the Duke of Argyll, manager of the Court interest in Scotland. He came out against the ministry in the general election of 1741 when, for once, the Scottish results bolstered the opposition rather than the government.

When parliament met Walpole found his position very precarious. Had his ministry been united he might have been able to control the situation. Instead disunity in ministerial ranks led to placemen becoming unreliable in divisions. As a result the Court failed to sustain a majority in the Commons, and after seven defeats Walpole resigned.

The two decades following the fall of Walpole, by contrast with his twenty years at the helm, were marked by the strife of factions competing for power. Walpole's resignation led to a jockeying for position in which the principal protagonists were Lords Bath and Carteret on the one hand and the Duke of Newcastle and his brother Henry Pelham on the other. Carteret had the backing of the king, as George demonstrated when he made him Earl of Granville. But the Pelhams had the support of the Commons, which they exploited in 1744 and, more dramatically, in 1746 when they resigned *en masse*. Although on the second occasion Granville tried to form a ministry it scarcely lasted two days. The king felt obliged to make Pelham prime minister. Eventually he came to accept the ministry of the Pelhamites, and their opponents, seeing no future in the reign of the ageing monarch, turned to his eldest son, Frederick Prince of Wales, in hopes of ousting the Pelhams when he came to the throne. Unfortunately for them Frederick died in 1751, upsetting all their calculations. The death of Henry Pelham in 1754, however, revived their aspirations. Again there was a jockeying for position between Newcastle, who succeeded his brother as prime minister, and rival factions. In 1756 William Pitt outmanoeuvered Newcastle and his henchman in the lower House, Henry Fox, gaining ascendancy in parliament. Once more George II was forced to dismiss a minister whom he wished to keep and to appoint a man who had the support of the Commons.

In May 1756 the French took Minorca from the British. The capture of the island caused consternation, with demands for scapegoats which blamed the prime minister as well as Admiral Byng who was held to be directly responsible for the loss. Pitt exploited the clamour to discredit Newcastle, who was deserted by his defenders in the Commons. As a result of the adverse reaction to the disaster in the Mediterranean the duke resigned. George II failed to find an alternative to offering office to his rival. Pitt tried to ingratiate himself with the king to obtain the necessary approval of the crown, but failed and was dismissed in April 1757. There ensued three months without a formal ministry due to the failure of any political combination to acquire the confidence of both king and Commons. It was not until Newcastle and Pitt agreed to combine in a joint administration that the essential sources of ministerial authority were combined also.

The Pitt–Newcastle administration presided over the most successful war fought by Britain during the eighteenth century. French possessions in two continents fell to her triumphant forces. In North America all of New France, from Canada to New Orleans, was acquired for the

British Empire. In India French influence was eliminated. Even the sugar island of Guadeloupe in the West Indies was gained in the 'wonderful year' of 1759.

The cost of these conquests, however, was huge. Taxpayers began to object to the demands made upon them to sustain the hostilities, and to suspect that Pitt was becoming over-ambitious in his war aims, especially when he demanded a declaration of war against Spain as well as France.

Among those who considered that the price of continued conflict was too high was George III, who succeeded as king on his grandfather's death in 1760. He determined to secure peace, a policy which led to the breakup of the ministry as Pitt resigned in 1761 to be followed by Newcastle a year later. Dispensing with the services of ministers who had led Britain to unprecedented successes in European and world affairs would have caused controversy anyway, just as Queen Anne's decision to get rid of the Whigs and ultimately to dismiss the Duke of Marlborough to pave the way for the Peace of Utrecht had done. What made George III's actions even more controversial was that he replaced them not with veteran or experienced rivals but with his 'dearest friend' Lord Bute. The constitutional propriety of promoting his personal tutor to the position of prime minister was called in question.

The king insisted that he had as much right to appoint Bute to the first lordship of the treasury as he had to dispose of any post in his service, since ministers were but his servants. His critics riposted that a prime minister could not be equated with household flunkeys since, unlike them, he had to be responsible to parliament. Had Bute been unable to command the confidence of the Commons then the king's claims would have been insupportable. But in fact the favourite did not lose a vote in parliament. A major difference between the politics behind the treaties of Utrecht and Paris was that George III, unlike Anne, did not have to call a general election to secure a majority for peace. The members returned in 1761 upheld his government through no fewer than five major ministerial changes. Bute resigned in 1763 not because he was defeated in parliament but because he had no stomach for the rough and tumble of politics. The young king felt he had been let down by his mentor. Out of office Bute became even more

The RECEPTION in 1760.

6 'The Reception in 1760' and 'The Reception in 1770': two prints depicting the popularity of King George III at his accession, and his unpopularity by 1770

controversial, being accused of exercising a secret influence behind the scenes until long after he enjoyed any real place in the royal counsels.

Bute indeed became one of the most maligned politicians of the century. The myth that he encouraged the king to act unconstitutionally by asserting the prerogative, though long dispelled, was potent in opposition circles at the time. The peace he negotiated with the French was assailed as a sell-out after Pitt's glorious conquests. Among his most outspoken critics was John Wilkes, who launched attacks on the unhappy prime minister in the *North Briton*. The forty-fifth number of this periodical became notorious when it published a thinly-veiled attack on the king himself.

Wilkes's outrageous journalism achieved notoriety because by the 1760s there was a nation-wide network of communications which he could exploit. An infrastructure of turnpike roads was then nearing completion. The principal provincial towns had their own newspapers, some of them boasting two and even three. These were read especially by an urban bourgeoisie which had expanded rapidly with the increase of trade and the rise of the professional classes. These provided Wilkes with a readership to which he appealed with his denunciations of the oligarchs who were in charge of the nation's affairs. Thus as the electoral system atrophied until it became less and less responsive to public opinion, voices were beginning to make themselves heard demanding a say in politics.

Wilkes drew attention to the widening gulf between these political worlds when he stood as a candidate for Middlesex. He was returned at the general election of 1768 only to be expelled from parliament, having previously been disqualified from sitting there as a seditious libeller. When a writ for a by-election to fill the vacancy was issued Wilkes stood and was returned, to be unseated again. This process occurred three times. On the first two occasions Wilkes was elected unopposed; on the third a government supporter stood against him. Although Wilkes polled more votes, his rival was declared duly elected by a majority of the House of Commons. Thus a chamber composed for the most part of men who sat for relatively small constituencies declared in effect who was to represent a populous county. Although technically the Commons had the constitutional right to do so, the Middlesex electors were outraged at this flouting of their wishes.

The Wilkites tried to channel these energies into the cause of parliamentary reform with the formation of the Society of Supporters of the Bill of Rights. The society, however, made little headway, partly because of quarrels among its leaders, but mainly because the classes to whom it appealed were not necessarily inclined towards political radicalism. On the contrary, those who could exercise the vote in the open constituencies did so in the general election of 1774 largely in favour of candidates who supported the government in its determination to suppress the rebellion in the American colonies.

Parliament was dissolved in 1774, a full year before a dissolution was required by the Septennial Act, in order to cash in on the apparent popularity of the government's stance with voters in the open constituencies. Dr Johnson's tract *Taxation no Tyranny* expressed a widespread British attitude. It was aimed as much against sympathisers with the colonists as at the American rebels, whose 'antipatriotic prejudices are the abortions of Folly impregnated with Faction'.

Attitudes towards the rebellious colonies hardened further in 1775 when the dispute deteriorated into open warfare. Support for the ministry's attempts to crush the rebellion was sustained through the Declaration of Independence, the defeat at Saratoga and the entry of the French into the war. But it could not survive the disaster of the surrender at Yorktown in 1781. North's ministry fell, to be replaced by the second administration of the Marquis of Rockingham, pledged to recognise the independence of the United States, a pledge carried out at the Treaty of Versailles in 1783.

Rockingham was committed to more than the recognition of American independence. He also dealt with serious unrest in Ireland and implemented a measure of economical reform.

The American war had vital implications for Ireland, since it was in a similar relationship with Britain to that of the colonies. The British parliament claimed the same rights of sovereignty over the Irish parliament as over the colonial assemblies, and in 1720 had passed an act asserting its right to legislate for Ireland. The Dublin parliament was also like a colonial assembly in that it represented a settler minority. The lower Houses in the colonies were elected by white adult males and did not represent blacks or Indians. The electorate for the Irish parliament was restricted in 1727 to Protestants, the great bulk of the population, Roman Catholics, who were frequently compared to native North Americans, being disfranchised. Since the Protestant ascendancy owed its constitutional rights, and ultimately its very existence, protected by an army of 12,000 men, to the British connexion, resistance to rule from London was less predictable from Ireland than it was from North America. Nevertheless it occurred. Resentment arose over the economic subservience to which Ireland was subjected by Britain. For instance, exports of cattle, sheep and wool to England were banned. The ban on the Irish woollen trade had ruined their staple product. Such measures affected the Protestants as much as they did the Catholics, if not more so. Objections to the way England used Ireland for its own purposes with scant regard for Irish interests could be aroused by particular issues. Jonathan Swift did this in his *Drapier's Letters* written against a scheme to issue large amounts of small change granted by the British government to an English projector in 1724. The opposition to it led to the recall of the patent and revealed that even Protestants in Ireland could demonstrate a kind of Irish patriotism.

'Patriot' indeed became the name of those who were prepared to speak out in the Dublin parliament against the domination of the British government. Patriots led by Henry Flood and Charles Lucas raised demands for more frequent parliaments early in George III's reign. Under the Hanoverians general elections had only been held in Ireland on their accessions. Although the proposal for more regular dissolutions was initially resisted it obtained enough support for the authorities to concede an Octennial Act in 1768. Following this concession Lord North's ministry became noticeably more sympathetic towards Irish grievances, offering partially to relax the barriers against trade. The offer was so strenuously opposed by British manufacturers, however, that North had substantially to withdraw it. Irish patriots then took a leaf out of the American colonists' book by organising a ban on British imports.

The entry of France into the War of American Independence threatened the security of Ireland, especially since 4,000 troops had been detached from the army there and sent to the American theatre. Awareness of the threat led Irishmen to raise volunteer corps for their own defence. Initially the Volunteer movement was exclusively Protestant, but eventually Catholics joined it too. From defence its energies were channelled into politics, with pressure brought to bear on the Irish parliament to demand free trade. A motion put before the

Dublin House of Commons to restrict supply to six months in an effort to persuade the British government to yield on this issue was carried. North, observing ominous parallels with American resistance, yielded. Jubilant at their success the Patriots, now led by Henry Grattan, went on in 1780 to demand legislative independence for the Irish parliament. When these demands were thwarted Grattan turned to the Volunteers, who convened a meeting at Dungannon in 1782 in support of his stance. Grattan and North were on a collision course when the prime minister fell from power over the American issue and was replaced by Rockingham, who was much more sympathetic to the Patriot cause. His ministry repealed the Act of 1720 which subjected Dublin to the Westminster parliament. Ireland became an independent kingdom, owing allegiance to the same king as Britain, but with its own parliament.

The attempts to make the Irish legislature less dependent upon the executive were paralleled in Britain by a campaign for economical reform. Economies in the administration, it was argued, would reduce the amount of patronage available to ministers and curtail their ability to employ it to build up a Court party in parliament. Rockingham advocated this approach, one of his connexion, John Dunning, moving the celebrated resolution in 1780 that 'the influence of the crown has increased, is increasing and ought to be diminished'. When the marquis came to power his secretary Edmund Burke introduced a bill which axed many posts, including the board of trade and the secretaryship for the colonies. The same reforming zeal inspired Clerke's Act, which forbade MPs from being government contractors, and Crewe's Act, which prohibited revenue officers from voting in parliamentary elections.

Other critics of the executive's grip on the Commons did not think that economical reform went far enough to relax it. One, Major Cartwright, actually advocated universal manhood suffrage. Another, the Reverend Christopher Wyvill, maintained that the preponderance of small boroughs made the Commons unrepresentative and that these should be offset by increasing the number of county seats to return more independent country gentlemen. In 1779 he founded the Yorkshire Association to press for this change.

Neither case made much headway in the 1780s. Cartwright's was scarcely helped when an aristocratic sympathiser put it to the House of

7   The Irish House of Commons, 1780

Lords in 1780 at a time when their lordships had to make their way into the chamber through a rioting mob. The Gordon riots put back the cause of franchise reform for a generation. They also indicated that the unenfranchised were as inclined to be reactionary as they were to be radical, since the rioters were protesting against a mild measure of relief for Catholics.

The campaign for the redistribution of seats from corrupt boroughs to counties gained more support. At one time the Association movement which sustained it came close to convening an alternative parliament. In the general election of 1784 Wyvill came out in favour of the younger Pitt. When the prime minister obtained a majority at the polls he honoured his debt to the Yorkshire Association by presenting a bill to take seventy-two seats from rotten boroughs and give them to counties. It was defeated by 293 votes to 149, not least because Pitt introduced it as a private member's bill and not as a ministerial measure. The ministry could normally command a majority after the election.

Before the dissolution of parliament, however, Pitt had sustained several defeats, one of them on a motion of no confidence. This rare occurrence in British political life arose from the jockeying for power which followed the death of Rockingham in July 1782. Charles James Fox and the Earl of Shelburne were the leading claimants to succeed him. George III, who had a personal aversion to Fox, chose Shelburne. Fox then threw in his lot with Lord North. This unexpected coalition between politicians who had previously been bitterly divided over the American war proved too strong for the ministry. Shelburne resigned and the king saw no real alternative at the time to appointing the Fox–North coalition to office under the nominal leadership of the Duke of Portland. George III waited, however, for the first opportunity to discredit and dismiss the coalition. It came in December 1783 when Fox put forward a bill setting up a board for the administration of India, appointments to and by which were to remain with the Commons and not be given to the crown. Denouncing this as an attack on the prerogative George put pressure upon the peers to oppose it. Upon its defeat in the Lords the king cashiered the coalition and appointed William Pitt to be prime minister, at the age of twenty-four the youngest in British history. But the coalition still controlled the Commons until a general election was called.

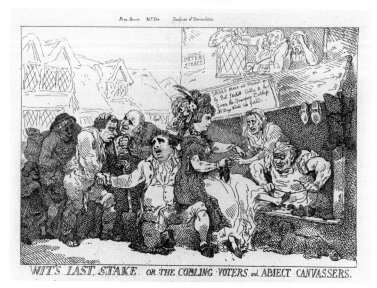

8 'Wit's Last Stake', a cartoon depicting the canvassing of the Westminster electors by Charles James Fox and his agents, including the publican Sam House and the Duchess of Devonshire, 1784

The elections of 1784 were the most significant of the Georgian era. That they would produce a majority for the new ministry was a foregone conclusion given the ability of the crown to influence the outcome, as Fox forlornly acknowledged when he speciously argued that George was obliged to let parliament run its full course of seven years. The limited impact of public opinion on overall election results or parliamentary proceedings is clear from the fact that members returned at the previous general election held four years earlier had upheld the very different ministries of North, Rockingham, Shelburne and Portland. That they continued to support Portland when George appointed Pitt, however, showed that there were limits to the crown's influence too. Although these could be overcome by fresh elections they nevertheless gave the king less room for manoeuvre than he had enjoyed at the outset of his reign. Since then the rise of party had reduced the options available to him. From the nucleus of the Rockingham connexion there had emerged a new Whig party. After the marquis's death this party had held together under Fox and been reinforced by his coalition with North. Coalition candidates in 1784 stood on the same platform, the defence of the rights of the Commons against the crown, and wore the same colours, buff and blue. Pittites also stood on the same platform, defence of the prerogative, and wore distinguishing colours of yellow or orange.

The polls thus witnessed a contest primarily between two parties for the first time since 1715. Both appealed to electoral opinion in the open constituencies. To Fox's chagrin the voters, where they could express a preference, showed that they preferred Pitt, the champion of the crown, to himself, the champion of the Commons. So far from offsetting the influence of the crown, therefore, as Fox had hoped, the results in the counties and cities actually reinforced it, giving Pitt a bigger majority than even his own supporters had predicted. They showed once again that public opinion was as inclined to be reactionary as it was to be radical.

One element in the electorate which was both radical and Pittite was the dissenting vote. Like Wyvill the dissenters also expected acknowledgment of their support, but the prime minister resisted their requests for repeal of the Test and Corporation Acts. Motions to repeal them were introduced into parliament three times between 1787 and 1790. They failed each time, albeit by only twenty votes on the second occasion. Moreover the minorities included the bulk of members for the larger constituencies, while the majority were composed predominantly of placemen and those who sat for small boroughs. Frustrated by their failure, dissenters, after supporting every administration since the accession of the House of Hanover, thereafter became associated with the opposition to Pitt and his successors and with the advocates of parliamentary reform.

Religion was thus at the centre of radical politics in the late eighteenth century. The connexion between religion and reform was revealed in 1772 with the failure of the Feathers Tavern petition. This was an attempt by Unitarians to persuade parliament to relax the Church of England's insistence on subscription to the Thirty-nine Articles. When it was defeated by 217 votes to 71 several Anglican ministers who had signed it left the church. They included John Jebb and Christopher Wyvill, who thereafter channelled their energies into reforming parliament. Jebb joined with Cartwright to found the Society for Constitutional Information in 1780, which advocated manhood suffrage, equal electoral districts and the secret ballot. Wyvill

went to the North Riding of Yorkshire to become a country gentleman
and to establish the Yorkshire Association.

These were signs that a consensus about the nature of the British
constitution was breaking down. For most of the century which
followed the Glorious Revolution commentators on its significance,
almost without exception, extolled it for having restored or established
the most perfect constitution man could devise. It had brought into
exact equilibrium the powers of monarchy, aristocracy and democracy.
Each in its pure form tended to degenerate, the first into tyranny, the
second into oligarchy and the third into anarchy. Yet properly balanced
they offset these tendencies. Crown and Lords together prevented the
Commons' anarchic proclivities; Crown and Commons resisted the
Lords' oligarchic aspirations; and Lords and Commons checked the
crown's tyrannical ambitions. Of course in practice abuses crept into
this theoretically perfect system. Thus corruption was employed by the
crown to corrode the independence of the Lords and Commons,
thereby reducing their capacity to check the monarchy. However, all
that was required to reverse these developments was to purge the
system of impurities, thereby restoring the pristine balance. Even the
Wilkites showed themselves in this respect to be reactionary rather
than radical. The very name of their Society of Supporters of the Bill
of Rights manifestly looked backwards to the allegedly ideal Revolution settlement.

Genuine radicalism arose with criticisms of the Revolution settlement itself, and not just of alleged abuses of it. Unitarians and
dissenters challenged the religious settlement of 1689. Richard Price
made this challenge quite explicit in *A Discourse on the Love of our
Country* wherein he argued that the Revolution, though it had replaced
hereditary with contractual kingship, had not gone far enough. The
much vaunted Toleration Act had not repealed the Test and Corporation Acts, so that Protestant dissenters were still denied civil
rights. At the same time the opportunity to expand the electorate had
been missed.

Price delivered his discourse to the Society for Commemorating the
Revolution on 4 November 1789, just a few months after the outbreak
of the French Revolution. He took the opportunity to welcome the
latter as promising a better outcome for France than 1688 had held out
for Britain.

This provoked Edmund Burke to riposte with his *Reflections on the Revolution in France* in which he praised the Glorious Revolution, claiming that Price had misrepresented it. The events of 1688–9 had restored and preserved the traditional institutions of England, while those of 1789 threatened to destroy those of the French. Contractual kingship had not been established, for only the slightest breach had been made in the hereditary principle to secure a Protestant succession. The preservation of the constitution in church and state required the safeguarding of the Anglican monopoly of power. Above all it was parliamentary and not popular sovereignty which had been upheld in 1689.

Burke's eulogy of the constitution prompted Thomas Paine to launch a scathing denunciation of it in *Rights of Man*, part one of which appeared in 1791, to be followed by a second part in 1792. Part two referred to the Bill of Rights as 'a bill of wrongs.' 'The defect,' maintained Paine, 'lies in the system. The foundation and the superstructure of the government is bad.' He asserted the sovereignty of the people against that of parliament. The representation of the people was much better catered for in revolutionary France than it was in England. Thus the number of French representatives was proportional to the number of taxable inhabitants. In Britain the tiny county of Rutland had two knights of the shire, as many as the populous county of Yorkshire, while Old Sarum, with hardly any inhabitants, returned two MPs and Manchester with over 60,000, sent none. 'Is there any principle in these things?' asked Paine. The answer was, of course, 'No.' The electoral system was not based on any rational principles, but had developed haphazardly over the centuries. This was what commended it to Burke.

The Scottish system, however, was less defensible, being more the artificial creation of the Union of 1707. Notoriously it was even less 'representative' than the English. Where advocacy of electoral reform rather lost its impetus in England before 1790, in Scotland it was still sustained. Petitions for reform of the burghs were presented to parliament in 1788, 1789, 1791 and 1792. 1792 also saw the establishment of reforming societies throughout Scotland, which held a General Convention of the Friends of the People in Edinburgh. Another convention held in the Scottish capital in 1793 drew delegates from England too.

9 The House of Commons, 1793–4

The English members of the Convention were sent by corresponding societies which had been formed in London, Sheffield and other provincial towns. These were the first genuinely artisan political societies in England. Radical politics now acquired a new social dimension. A ruling class frightened by the French Revolution was terrified of the prospect of British 'Jacobins' using these societies as revolutionary cells. They were particularly apprehensive of the widespread diffusion of part two of Paine's *Rights of Man*, a cheap edition of which sold 200,000 copies. It was regarded as so republican in spirit, so hostile to monarchy and the hereditary principle, that Paine was prosecuted for seditious libel and, after he fled to France, convicted in his absence. The fact that his work circulated amongst the societies made them appear especially seditious to the governing classes. They closed ranks against this threat. In 1794 conservative Whigs led by the Duke of Portland went over to the government. The Pitt–Portland ministry clamped down on anything perceived to be 'Jacobinism'. Thus the Habeas Corpus Act was suspended in 1794, and the following year public meetings were banned unless approved by magistrates. The courts were also used to crush the 'British Jacobins', who rather invited judicial attention at the Convention held in Edinburgh in 1793 by sending fraternal greetings to French politicians. Since Britain went to war with France that year such activities could be construed as treason. The Scottish judiciary reacted by sentencing delegates found guilty of abetting the enemy to transportation. Charges brought against English radicals, however, resulted in their acquittal.

Although it is grotesque to describe the reaction to radicalism as 'Pitt's Reign of Terror', the attempt to suppress radical societies did betray a determination to eradicate criticism of the constitution. The ruling classes were not prepared to succumb to demands for constitutional change from below. Even Charles James Fox, leader of the Whigs who remained in opposition, while he opposed the suppression was appalled by the first part of *Rights of Man* and could not bring himself to read the second part.

The policy of suppression proved to be effective. There are few signs of radicalism for the rest of the period of the wars with revolutionary and Napoleonic France. Political agitation can be detected behind the naval mutinies at the Nore and Spithead in 1797, the food riots of 1800–1, and the Despard conspiracy of 1802. How far this was the tip of an iceberg of radical activity forced to go 'underground' and to become more 'revolutionary' by the clamp-down is debatable. The mutinies and the riots were inspired by genuine economic grievances which radicals tried to exploit. The Despard conspiracy was genuine enough, but was the English arm of a primarily Irish plot. In Ireland revolutionaries could count on the sympathy of a substantial section of the population, an essential ingredient for sustaining a clandestine revolutionary movement. In England no such favourable circumstances existed. On the contrary, the bulk of the English rallied to the government in the 1790s. A popular reaction set in before the outbreak of war with France which identified radicalism with 'Jacobinism'. In 1791, a 'church and king' mob demolished the house and laboratory of the Unitarian Joseph Priestley in Birmingham. In 1792 associations to defend 'liberty and property' against 'republicans and levellers' sprang into existence. Although the government encouraged their formation they also represented a spontaneous reaction. As in the Gordon riots and the general election of 1784, wherever public opinion made itself felt it manifested a propensity toward reaction as well as towards radicalism. The Foxite rump of the Whigs who remained in opposition fared badly in the open constituencies at the polls in 1796. Their claim that the constitution was more in danger from the crown and the army than it was from the French found little support amongst the electors.

Not that the constitution remained frozen during Pitt's first ministry. On the contrary, there were perceptible changes involving the monarchy, the executive's relations with parliament, and above all Britain's connection with Ireland.

George III's determination to find a prime minister with whom he could work and who at the same time could command the confidence of the House of Commons kept him in the thick of the political dogfight from his accession until the appointment of the younger Pitt and the outcome of the 1784 election brought about the ideal combination. Then in 1788 the king suffered the first attack of a debilitating illness diagnosed in modern times as porphyria, the symptoms of which include mental derangement. Clearly unfit to rule, the king had to be replaced by a regent. The regency crisis created an opportunity for the opposition led by Charles James Fox to press the claims of their ally the Prince of Wales. But when the king recovered in 1789 before they could capitalise on his illness it condemned them to the opposition benches and cemented Pitt's ascendancy. At the same time it left George disinclined to undertake the routine business of government. As he informed Pitt he would 'only keep that superintending eye which can be effected without labour or fatigue'. The disengagement of the king from day-to-day duties was a major step in the elevation of the crown above the political fray. During the American war and its immediate aftermath George III had been an active participant in politics and had incurred a great deal of unpopularity. Pitt's triumph and the king's illness began the process whereby the crown became a national symbol rather than a focus for partisan loyalties.

Pitt assisted the process whereby the influence of the crown declined by eliminating sinecures from the administration in the interests of economic reform. The result was a diminution of the executive's ability to control the Commons, the number of placemen in the lower House being much reduced by his retrenchment. Pitt also persuaded the king to raise more men to the peerage than his Hanoverian predecessors had done. George I and George II, conscious of the shock created by Queen Anne's ennoblement of twelve peers at once in 1712, and also determined to uphold the dignity of the peerage, kept the number of noblemen more or less steady. After 1790 the numbers rose, making the House of Lords a larger and less controllable chamber.

But the biggest change involved Ireland. The impact of the French Revolution on the Irish situation was far more of a threat to the British government than it was in England. Although the constitution of 1782 gave legislative independence to Ireland it did not satisfy all the demands of the Volunteers. They went on to agitate for parliamentary reform, agitation taken up by the Society of United Irishmen, formed in 1791. Their advocacy of universal suffrage included Catholics, showing that the society lived up to its name. The Dublin parliament responded in 1793 by granting a Catholic Relief Act which gave Catholics the vote but not seats in parliament. Those who supported the society's aims were ultimately hoping for independence from Britain, as the British government realised when it suppressed the United Irishmen in 1794. The more determined of them founded the United Irish Society the following year. The French tried to exploit Irish aspirations in their own struggle with the British. They attempted a landing in Bantry Bay in December 1796, while expectations of another invasion in 1798 inspired an insurrection in Ireland. Pitt was converted to the view that the only safe solution was to incorporate Ireland into the United Kingdom, a view shared by the Protestant ascendancy which agreed to the Act of Union in 1800. This added 100 Irish seats to the 558 British seats in the House of Commons. It was agreed that the thirty-two Irish counties should retain two members each, leaving only 36 borough seats. Since there had been 117 boroughs represented in the defunct Irish parliament there had to be considerable disfranchisement and some reorganisation. Proprietors of disfranchised boroughs were compensated by the treasury to the tune of £1,400,000.

3

Nineteenth-century Britain

The Act of Union of 1800 was a greater turning point in the history of Britain than either the French Revolution or the Reform Act of 1832. It ushered in the nineteenth century by incorporating Ireland into the United Kingdom and thereby put Irish problems at the top of the agenda of British politics, not least because the 100 members returned to Westminster from the province were determined to keep them there.

Sixty-four of these MPs sat for the thirty-two counties. As in England the franchise was the possession of a forty-shilling freehold. Since owners of such freeholds were relatively rare in Ireland, however, a much larger proportion of the county electorates consisted of leaseholders for lives, making electors more dependent upon landlords than English voters were. The most crucial difference, however, was the fact that nearly 80 per cent of the population of Ireland was Catholic. Although Catholics could not legally stand for parliament until 1829, they could vote in parliamentary elections. The rest of the electorate was divided between the established Church of Ireland and various other Protestant denominations of which the Presbyterians in Ulster were the largest.

Where mainland Britain was becoming increasingly industrialised in the early nineteenth century, Ireland's economy, paradoxically, was becoming more agrarian. Although urbanisation was occurring, especially with the growth of Belfast, nevertheless the country remained overwhelmingly rural, and the main industry, textiles, was in serious decline. The social structure of Ireland thus remained relatively unchanged by economic developments. Large landowners, often

Protestant and absentee, leased land to tenants, usually Catholic. This aggravated tensions between landlord and tenant, partly through ethnic and religious differences, but mainly because the landed elite claimed ownership by British statute law, with all the rights of proprietorship, while the Irish tenants regarded their customary tenure as a kind of joint ownership. Social conflict in Ireland revolved principally around these rural tensions.

In Britain, by contrast, urbanisation was creating new tensions, with society increasingly polarising along class lines. The making of the working class came about with the rapid growth of the industrial towns after 1800. During the 1820s the population of Bradford in the West Riding of Yorkshire increased by a phenomenal 65 per cent, while in the same decade Leeds grew by 47 per cent and Birmingham by 40 per cent. Working-class aspirations were articulated by those who organised corresponding societies, trades unions and ultimately Chartism. Although the Chartist movement was the first working-class campaign one must be careful not to regard the lower strata of society as monolithic. Much of the political agitation of the times was organised by traditional craftsmen such as the shoemaker Thomas Hardy. Even with the emergence of factory workers, a distinction must be drawn at all times between the artisans or 'labour aristocracy' and the mass of labourers.

Feeding the growing masses was a major problem. In these decades Britain changed from being a net exporter of agricultural produce to being a net importer. Poor harvests, as in the 1790s, caused prices to rise to unprecedented heights and caused considerable distress. It took time for the agricultural sector of the economy to adjust to new demands. Unlike Ireland, however, which became over-dependent upon the potato crop, with disastrous results in the 1840s, people in Britain did not actually starve. On the contrary, after the disruption caused by the French wars, agricultural productivity kept prices reasonably stable during the 1820s, leading to a rise in real wages. This in turn led to consumer demand for manufactured articles.

How far this stimulated an 'industrial revolution' depends on what meaning is attached to that overworked term. If it is used as a shorthand for a dramatic transformation of the economy from household to factory units of mass production then hardly anything of the sort occurred before 1830. For one thing the basic infrastructure of

10   Glasgow in 1835

the economy, in terms such as the efficiency of the agricultural sector, the improvement of communications by turnpike roads and canals, the availability of credit and the mobility of labour, was much more advanced by 1780 than is allowed for by those who see changes taking place thereafter as revolutionary. For another, the rate of industrialisation was slower than the term implies. To be sure, some industries became concentrated into factories, such as the manufacture of cotton textiles in Manchester and other Lancashire towns and of woollens in the West Riding of Yorkshire. Even this did not take place overnight, but gradually between 1780 and 1830. Elsewhere industry, even the metalware production of Birmingham and Sheffield, continued to be carried out in small workshops.

Nevertheless the growth of these industrial centres in the midlands and the north did significantly affect social trends. A greater proportion of a growing population was concentrated in them than had been the case previously. Some effects of this were definitely detrimental. Disease and squalor caused by overcrowding led to horrific death rates. Cyclical unemployment created problems which a poor relief system designed to deal with the chronic underemployment of an agricultural economy could not solve. Added to this was the redundancy of skills such as hand-loom weaving which declined as the textile industry was merchandised. On the credit side, however, wages in manufacturing were higher than in agriculture, which is why men migrated to industrial towns. It is a myth that they were forced off the land by the enclosure movement, as agriculture continued to be labour intensive until well into the nineteenth century. Since there was scarcely any mechanisation of farming, while the amount of land under cultivation increased, one must look to 'pull' rather than to 'push' factors to account for the migration to the towns. Moreover although technology caused redundancies it also created new forms of employment, for instance in the construction and running of railways which spread rapidly after the opening of the Stockton to Darlington line in 1825.

Just as the Tudor and Stuart poor law system had not been designed to cope with the economic and social problems of an industrial society so the mediaeval and early modern provisions for parliamentary representation had not been intended to accommodate the political aspirations of an increasingly urbanised kingdom. The landed elite stood up well to the challenges posed by the emergence of the urban middle and working classes. It is remarkable that the aristocracy dominated the national government of Britain down to the First World War. Victorian cabinet ministers were predominantly peers, from Lord Grey's cabinet, arguably the most aristocratic of the nineteenth century, to Lord Salisbury's. Landlords were a majority of members of parliament until 1885 when, at the first general election to be held after the third Reform Act, there was a sudden drop in the proportion of landed gentry in the Commons. They were not replaced by industrialists, however, so much as by professional men. It could be that this change marked a political adjustment to economic changes brought about by the agricultural depression and the relatively diminished significance of the landed interest in the economy. More likely, though, it represented a social phenomenon. Membership of parliament was probably becoming less attractive to country gentlemen who had previously found it a congenial club and a boost to their local status. With the growth of parties and party discipline, and lengthening of sessions, the increase in the amount of parliamentary time demanded by government, in a word the professionalisation of politics, the world of Westminster was increasingly alien to amateur and welcoming to career politicians. Perhaps the last straw for many was that after the Reform Act of 1884 they had to solicit the votes of agricultural labourers.

Although urbanisation and then industrialisation threatened the coherence of county communities, landowners nevertheless survived as leaders in rural Britain. They contrived to do this despite the fact that a County Councils Act of 1888 seemed to threaten their rural hegemony. This measure, introduced by a Conservative government, replaced the quarter sessions, at which the magistrates administered the affairs of the counties, with elected bodies. And yet the anticipated social revolution did not happen in the shires. On the contrary, the aristocracy and gentry continued to rule them, though now as county councillors rather than as justices of the peace. Thus the Marquis of Bath continued to preside over the affairs of Wiltshire albeit as chairman of the county council rather than of the quarter sessions. Most county councillors were returned unopposed at election after election. The ascendancy of the landed elite was not even challenged by the Local Government Act of 1894 which set up parish, rural and urban district councils, although that was introduced by a Liberal government.

The landed elite survived as a ruling class because it adapted itself to changing social and economic conditions. The classic instances of its adaptability are the various reform acts which increased the electorate and extended the boundaries of political participation. But another reason why the governing classes never became isolated from the rest of society in Britain was that they rarely used their potential power solely to further their own interests at the expense of others.

Indeed the state, even in the seventeenth and eighteenth centuries, did not crudely protect the landed interest. The prohibition on the export of raw wool, for instance, was disadvantageous to farmers, who formed a substantial section of that interest. Yet it was sustained by the state, which penalised the smuggling of wool for the protection of the woollen cloth manufacturers. The prosperity of the manufacturing section of the economy was held to be a major objective of policy even if it adversely affected agriculture. Of course it could be, and was, argued that it was to the best interest of the agriculturalist that a predominantly rural workforce was kept in employment by protecting it from foreign competition. Otherwise unemployed weavers would be a charge on the poor rate which every landowner paid. Nevertheless state power was used directly to benefit an interest other than that of land.

The prime example of the state protecting the landed interest was the enactment of the Corn Laws. These became a target of complaint from merchants and manufacturers who criticised them for being a blatant abuse of power by the landowners who exercised authority through parliament. After their repeal in 1846, however, it became hard to sustain such criticisms. On the contrary, the prevalent ideology of *laisser-faire* allowed any interest to function free of state control in theory. It is true that enough exceptions were found to this rule in practice to raise doubts about the commitment of Victorians to the concept. A series of factory acts, public health acts, prison acts, railway, gas and water acts, for example, demonstrated a willingness to use the powers of the state to regulate social and economic activities. Between 1847 and 1853 three major enactments restricted the hours worked in factories to a maximum of ten a day between 6.00 a.m. and 6.00 p.m. Yet the advocates of these measures themselves assumed that the onus was on them to demonstrate a moral case for interference.

The ideology that society was best left to regulate itself unless morality justified intervention was at a philosophical level a blend of political economy and religious evangelicalism. As an economic theory it drew on the contributions of economists from Adam Smith to Thomas Chalmers. Although 'the dismal science', as economics was dubbed, can be seen as a purely secular study, it contained a strong religious element too. Man 'in seeking his own gain', observed Smith, 'is led by an invisible hand to promote an end which was no part of his intention'. Chalmers thought that the indiscriminate relief of poverty by the state actually thwarted God's will. He accepted Thomas Malthus's gloomy prediction that population grew geometrically while resources increased arithmetically until demographic pressures overtook agricultural productivity only to be reversed by the calamities of disease, famine or war. It was therefore the duty of the state to prevent rather than to encourage the growth of population. Since the poor laws did not discourage paupers from marrying and having children they should be made harsher to prevent the poor from behaving fecklessly. This would encourage sexual restraint and thereby Christian morality. Such thinking lay behind the Poor Law Amendment Act of 1834.

At a more popular level *laisser-faire* could be characterised as a philosophy of enlightened self-interest. Thousands of Victorians who never read the works of political economists bought such best-selling books as *Self-Help* by Samuel Smiles, published in 1859, and Lord Macaulay's *History of England*. 'The spirit of self-help is the root of all genuine growth in the individual', asserted Smiles, 'and, exhibited in the lives of the many, it constitutes the true source of national vigour and strength.' A basic message of Macaulay's *History* was that 'no ordinary misfortune, no ordinary misgovernment, will do so much to make a nation wretched as the constant effort of every man to better himself will do to make a nation prosperous. It has often been found that profuse expenditure, heavy taxation, absurd commercial restrictions... have not been able to destroy capital as fast as the exertions of private citizens have been able to create it.'

Among the commercial restrictions he presumably had in mind were customs duties. In the interests of free trade these were progressively

11   The entrance of Queen Victoria and Prince Albert at the opening of the Great Exhibition

reduced until in 1860 Gladstone's budget left only fifty commodities liable to them. In the same year a free trade treaty was negotiated with France. The Victorian state played a positive as well as a negative function in promoting free trade, employing the royal navy to protect merchant shipping around the globe.

The state also positively encouraged manufactures, as its role in promoting the Great Exhibition of 1851, the greatest Victorian celebration of industry, demonstrated. The inspiration for the 'Great Industrial Exhibition of All Nations' came from Prince Albert. Its celebrated symbol, the Crystal Palace, was designed by Paxton who had previously been employed by the Duke of Devonshire to make huge greenhouses at Chatsworth. Queen Victoria opened the Exhibition, accompanied by the full paraphernalia of a state occasion, with the pursuivants of arms – Blue Mantle, Rouge Dragon, Portcullis and Rouge Croix – the heralds of Windsor, York, Richmond and Lancaster, Gold and Silver Sticks in Waiting, and so on. There were peers among the jurors who judged the exhibits and awarded medals. Six of the thirty juries had aristocrats as chairmen or deputy chairmen. There were even lords among the exhibitors, including the Marquis of Breadalbane who exhibited specimens from his mines, quarries and woods and the wool of a bison. But these were a mere handful, outnumbered many times even by women exhibitors among the thousands whose entries were accepted. The manufacturers and inventors were overwhelmingly the middle classes of mid-Victorian Britain. They included many who were, or became, household names, such as Chubb the locksmith, Fry the chocolatier, Lambert and Butler the tobacconists, Brown and Polson, Colman, Reckitt, Fortnum and Mason, and Huntley and Palmer. Yet the class structure was steadfastly upheld. At the opening only those with season tickets, three guineas for 'gentlemen', two for 'ladies', were admitted to the ceremony. Thereafter the public was allowed in at different prices on different days: five shillings; two shillings and sixpence; and one shilling. Thus the upper, middle and lower classes saw the Exhibition on separate occasions. On the first 'shilling day' over 60,000 people attended. Between the opening on 1 May and the closing on 15 October over 6 million paid entrance fees and filed through the narrow doorways. Although this figure included multiple and foreign visitors it was still a stupendous proportion of a total British population of about 21 million recorded in the census of 1851.

Yet although the Exhibition announced the arrival of the industrial sector of the economy on the national stage it did not play as dominant a role in the political arena as the commercial interests. In part this was due to the fact that it was scattered throughout many provincial centres and was not concentrated in the capital as so many banking and insurance businesses were. Thus industry was more remote from the corridors of power than was finance. Another reason why manufacturing never acquired the clout in Britain that its reputation as the first industrial nation might have led one to expect was that it began to be outstripped by foreign competitors after about 1870. In response manufacturers began to clamour for protection, which was contrary to the prevailing philosophy of free trade.

When the government refused to respond to their pleas they took steps to rescue themselves from the effects of foreign competition by cutting the wages of their employees. A classic example of this self-protection occurred in Bradford in 1890. The West Riding had been very badly affected by the McKinley tariff in the United States. Samuel Cunliffe Lister, owner of one of the biggest mills in the city, retaliated by cutting the wages of his weavers by three shillings a week. They responded by going on strike in December. They were out for four bitter months, until the strike was broken. Few had been members of the woollen workers' union at the outset, but the strike was a great boost to the labour movement in Yorkshire, and the main reason why Bradford was chosen as the venue for the launching of the Independent Labour Party in 1893. Other groups of workers, finding themselves adversely affected by the depression, organised themselves into trades unions in these years. In 1893 there were about one and a half million trade unionists; by 1900 there were over 2 million. Most of the increase occurred in the so-called 'new unions' which organised workers by industries, such as the dockers and the gas workers, rather than by trades. They called upon the state to intervene in industrial relations to secure better conditions for their members. The late Victorian state, however, was as deaf to their appeals as it was to that of the employers who sought protection from competition.

Meanwhile the City reasserted its economic importance in government circles against the industrial sector. The treasury, the Bank of England and the City's financial institutions came together in late Victorian Britain to forge a formidable alliance in favour of free trade. It was in these years that the British state came to value the 'invisible' imports of the City more than the visible exports of the industrial towns. By the turn of the century the ruling class consisted of an alliance between the old landed elite and the new insurance and financial sector of the City. Their members joined the same clubs and sent their sons to the same public schools. They shared an ethos which, far from being sympathetic to the industrialists, was positively disdainful of manufacturers. This disdain has been identified as a crucial element in the decline of the industrial spirit in the last hundred years. Manufacturers in turn came to feel inferior in status. Instead of aspiring to ever greater feats of entrepreneurship, it has been claimed that they sought to send their sons to public schools and university, and to set themselves up as landed gentlemen in the countryside. Thus Armstrong, the Krupp of Victorian Tyneside, acquired Bamburgh Castle and built Cragside, while Samuel Cunliffe Lister, the Bradford millowner, bought 30,000 acres of Yorkshire estate when property values slumped in the 1880s and was ennobled as Baron Masham. How typical these industrial magnates were is questionable. Actual entry into the landed elite was remarkably restricted in Victorian Britain.

Most sons of manufacturers inherited the family firm rather than a country mansion.

Whether or not there has been a decline of the industrial spirit is therefore debatable. That there has been a decrease in religious sentiment, or at least in formal observance of religion, is indisputable. In 1851 there was a unique religious census of those who attended services on 30 March. The results shocked contemporaries. In England and Wales roughly seven and a quarter million attendances were recorded out of a total population of nearly 18 million. Massaging the figures to give the best results for the churches and chapels indicates that about 40 per cent of those who could have attended did not do so. The Church of England was particularly perturbed by the findings. Some two-thirds of its pews were unoccupied that Sunday, while nearly half of those who attended services did so in Roman Catholic or nonconformist churches. In Scotland churchgoing was apparently more prevalent than in England, some one and three-quarter million attendances being recorded out of a population of nearly 3 million. The established Church of Scotland, however, had an even smaller share of the worshippers there than the Anglicans in England, barely a third of the total. The rest mainly attended the Free Church and the United Presbyterian Church, both seceders from the establishment, which had managed to sustain their congregations.

The attendance figures were lowest in the working-class districts of industrial towns. Both church and chapel failed to accommodate the workers of Clydeside, Tyneside, the West Riding of Yorkshire and the cotton district of Lancashire. It was not through want of trying, but the clergy, especially of the established churches, were inevitably middle class by background and failed to appreciate working-class attitudes. Only Catholic priests born in Ireland appear to have shared the outlook of their flocks. Their main problem was finding room for their congregations, since there were only 186,111 seats in Catholic churches. Some Anglican parishes would have had even more difficulty accommodating the masses had they chosen to attend. In Bradford, Yorkshire, for example, the parish church catered for a population of 78,332 people with 1,400 sittings of which all but 200 were rented.

The religious census galvanised the churches into a building campaign funded by voluntary contributions which drastically increased the accommodation for worshippers, leaving behind Gothic structures which are among the most prominent visible remains of the Victorian era in modern Britain. Between 1851 and 1880 the provision of sittings in the industrial region of Lancashire was augmented 106 per cent by the Baptists, 90 per cent by the Roman Catholics, 85 per cent by the Wesleyans and 39 per cent by the Anglicans, the last in absolute terms being far and away the greatest, from 133,351 to 185,630, which was more than all the others combined. Meanwhile, however, the total population of Britain increased by approximately 30 per cent to 25,974,339. Churches and chapels had to run faster just to stay in the same place.

And yet despite the census shocking contemporaries, Victorian Britain was a religious society. Attendance figures of the order recorded in 1851 would need no massaging to delight Christians in the late twentieth century. Today's secular society is a recent development. Those who were absent from their devotions on 30 March 1851 could scarcely have been diverting themselves in public assemblies since the laws were very strict about Sunday entertainments. Even the Crystal Palace was not allowed to open on what many Victorians called the 'Sabbath'.

Lord Palmerston, though scarcely a model of piety in his personal life, was typically Victorian in his attitude towards religion when he viewed it as a means of social control. He disregarded the outcome of the religious census, being convinced that the established church catered for two-thirds of churchgoers and 'dissenters', as he continued to call them, for one-third. In his view high church Anglicanism, with its stress on the creed and the liturgy, appealed to the upper classes, while low church or evangelical Anglicanism, with its insistence on regeneration, was more appealing to the middle and lower classes. As prime minister he consulted the evangelical peer Lord Shaftesbury, who was also his son-in-law, about the promotion of bishops, preferring low church clergy, believing that high church men were out of touch with the masses. The fact that a few high church Anglicans were converted to Roman Catholicism at the height of the so-called Oxford movement in the 1840s confirmed him in this belief. While Palmerston's attitude towards religious affiliations and ecclesiastical sociology was a trifle cavalier, there was a sense in which he had a point. Asked to profess a denomination most people in Victorian England would probably have said 'C of E', which was one reason why

12   The census enumerator in a Gray's Inn Lane tenement

proposals to get them to express their religious allegiance in the 1861 census were resisted, not least by nonconformists.

The census thus reflected social values as well as registering vital statistics. The introduction to the report of 1851 made this quite clear when it asserted that there was a strong desire in Britain for 'the possession of an entire house'. As the anonymous author explained, 'it throws a sharp, well-defined circle round his family and hearth – the shrine of his sorrows, joys and meditations.' So many Victorian values are encapsulated here. The imagined aspirant for home ownership is a man, for this was a male-dominated society. The home has become the centre of a domestic cult. It is presided over by what the census enumerators termed 'the head of the household' and what others called 'the breadwinner'. Home was also 'a woman's place', where like a superior domestic servant the wife played the role of 'the angel of the house'. The domestic ideal was enshrined in the Victorian invention of Christmas. This family festival, with the Christmas tree introduced by Prince Albert and the dinner popularised by Charles Dickens in *A Christmas Carol*, reinforced the myth that people lived in a house, however humble, presided over by a patriarchal husband and father.

This aspiration was in fact realised by only a minority of upper- and middle-class married men and women. The rich man in his castle, like the Duke of Northumberland at Alnwick, certainly owned it. Most of the rural gentry also owned theirs. But below that level of society the vast majority of houses, from the suburban villas to the back-to-backs of the industrial north, were rented. Most single men even in the professions rented part of a house rather than owning one entirely. Almost all working men, at least below the 'labour aristocracy', single or married, rented accommodation. Many men and women in domestic service lived in the house of a married couple, catering to their needs and those of their children. Between 1851 and 1871 the numbers of such servants increased by some 60 per cent as mid-Victorian prosperity enabled more and more middle-class households to employ them. The proportion of single-parent families revealed by analyses of census schedules was about the same then as now, though the cause was the death rather than the divorce of a spouse. Many women died in childbirth. Those who survived childbearing were prone to survive their husbands too. As widows they were not always maintained in the bosom of their families. On the contrary many spent their declining years in institutions such as the poor house or private homes.

In this respect Victoria was typical of the age to which she gave her name for she became a widow in 1861. Her prolonged grief after the death of the Prince Consort led her to become something of a recluse. She could not bear to be in Buckingham Palace, and spent her time between Windsor Castle, Osborne on the Isle of Wight and Balmoral in Scotland. Her psychological inability to bring herself to take part in state functions such as the opening of parliament caused murmurings in the press. But the degree to which criticism of the monarch veered towards condemnation of monarchy itself in the 1860s and 1870s has been much exaggerated. And when she eventually emerged from her prolonged mourning Victoria became one of the most popular monarchs in British history. The enthusiasm for the jubilees of 1887 and 1897 surpassed all previous criticisms of the ruling dynasty. By her death in 1901 the crown had never been more firmly entrenched as an institution.

The stage management of the jubilees invented a tradition that the British had always been good at putting on state spectacles. In fact earlier efforts of this kind had been inferior to those of the continental monarchies. It was really in the late nineteenth and early twentieth

13   Osborne House, Isle of Wight

centuries, as the other monarchies went into decline, that the British made a major effort to sustain the image of the crowned heads by organising spectacular royal occasions, the coronation of Edward VII being among the more lavish. This helped to assure the popularity of the monarchy and with it the whole social hierarchy with which it was associated. One of the reasons why the hereditary peerage still exerts influence over public life is because it is underpinned by royalty. The special place of the royal family in British public opinion has been a major reason why a ruling class which has long since ceased to enjoy any great economic importance nevertheless stubbornly survives in the twentieth century.

That it survived the nineteenth, a century of unprecedented demographic, industrial and urban growth, is a striking indication of the resilience of British institutions to social and economic change. Despite tensions between church and chapel there was no counterpart in Victorian Britain of the violent anticlericalism witnessed on the continent. Nor was there a radical movement which came near to threatening the security of the state.

4

From Pitt to Palmerston

When Pitt indicated that he intended the Act of Union to give Catholics full emancipation George III refused to concede it. The king's refusal led the prime minister to resign in 1801. Pitt's resignation appears to demonstrate that the crown retained ultimate authority despite recent constitutional changes. Certainly to George it was a matter of principle that he had sworn to uphold the Protestant constitution in church and state, and he regarded Catholic emancipation as a breach of his coronation oath. Yet had Pitt chosen to resist the royal will on this issue it is hard to see how the king could have withstood him. The ministry of Henry Addington which replaced him was very narrowly based and really only lasted as long as the former premier refused to oppose it. When Pitt did offer opposition, Addington fell and was replaced by his predecessor. Pitt's second ministry came to an unexpected end in 1806 with his early death at the age of forty-five.

Pitt died in the middle of the most titanic struggle Britain ever fought against a foreign foe. The war declared by France in 1793 lasted twenty-two years, with only one short breathing space, the Peace of Amiens negotiated in 1801, which broke down in 1803. Although the wars against Louis XIV had been nearly as protracted they had not seen Britain virtually isolated and in serious danger of a French invasion. By the time of Pitt's death the threat of invasion had been eliminated by the navy, principally by Nelson's victory at Trafalgar in 1805. But the prospect of beating France was still very uncertain. It was to take over nine more years for a coalition to be constructed against Napoleon which finally defeated him at the battle of Waterloo in 1815.

14   King George III at Windsor, 1807

Pitt laid the fiscal foundations for this colossal war effort with his financial measures. The total cost of the wars came to £1,039,000,000. In real terms in the last ten years of the conflict the government spent over three times as much per annum on the war effort than had been expended in the War of American Independence. Yet where earlier wars had been largely financed by loans on the security of deferred taxes, Pitt took steps to ensure that these were paid for largely from current taxation. This involved increasing the rates of existing taxes and introducing new ones, most notably the first income tax raised in 1799. Although the tax burden was unprecedentedly heavy it provoked remarkably few complaints, another sign that the British government could depend upon the support of the bulk of the population during the conflicts with revolutionary and Napoleonic France.

After the wars, however, the consensus which they stimulated broke down. A proposal to continue the income tax was defeated in parliament by 238 votes to 201 in 1816. Large-scale rural riots occurred that year, to be followed by the Spa Fields riot of 1817. These disturbances, provoked in part by a post-war recession, culminated in the so-called 'massacre' of Peterloo in 1819. Crowds assembled in St Peter's Fields in Manchester to hear 'Orator' Hunt advocate parliamentary reform were dispersed by militia and regular troops, with the result that many were seriously injured while eleven were killed. The government reacted to the unrest with repressive measures reminiscent of Pitt's in the 1790s. The Habeas Corpus Act was suspended in 1817, and the Six Acts were introduced in 1819. Three sought to prevent radicals from organising meetings or preparing for insurrection, two curbed the press, and one restricted the legal rights of those charged with seditious conspiracy or libel. The Whigs offered no opposition to the bill preventing civilians from taking part in paramilitary activities. They appreciated that nobody in parliament was in favour of allowing the formation, drilling and arming of private armies. But they opposed the other five bills, forcing sixteen divisions before they passed the Commons. Though they passed with comfortable majorities the issues which they raised polarised parliament into distinct parties for and against the government's suppression of radicals.

Nor were the divisions confined to parliament. The Peterloo massacre divided English society, with petitions and mass meetings being organised for and against the stance taken by the authorities. Again it could not be presumed that the radicals had the bulk of public opinion automatically on their side.

In 1820, however, an episode arose which showed that the established powers could not take for granted the allegiance of the majority. This was the vexed question of Queen Caroline. In 1795 the Prince of Wales had married Princess Caroline of Brunswick. Within a year of the wedding, although they shared Carlton House, they led separate lives, which led to scandal-mongering in the press. In 1814 Caroline went abroad and passed out of the English gossip columns, though she provided plenty of copy for continental journalists. The prince pressed for evidence to obtain a divorce, but this was not forthcoming before his father's death in 1820, when he became King George IV and the princess, to his and the ministry's embarrassment, became his queen. The new king refused to have his wife's name included in the Prayer Book to be prayed for along with himself. Ministers desperately tried to find a solution which would prevent Caroline being recognised as queen and yet provide her with compensation for the loss of the royal title. In the midst of this crisis she arrived in England to a tumultuous reception, which portended the popular reaction to the episode.

The government led by Lord Liverpool introduced a bill which deprived Caroline of her entitlement to the crown, and incidentally divorced her from the king for 'licentious, disgraceful and adulterous intercourse in various places and countries'. The bill floundered in the Lords, and Liverpool felt obliged to withdraw it. George, not surprisingly, was furious. It seemed at one time that he might turn to the Whigs to rescue him from the impasse, but they had been carried along on the wave of public opinion in favour of the queen and were in no position to help. Prints depicted the portly king at his most corpulent and beastly, while crowds cheered Caroline wherever she appeared.

When the Whigs tried to follow up the withdrawal of the Bill of Pains and Penalties with demands that the queen be reinstated in the liturgy and with a motion of censure on the government, they were rebuffed by huge majorities. The independents were too wary of the popular emotions unleashed by the trial, and the way the Whigs were exploiting it, to divide against the ministry. The crisis ended with the sudden death of the queen in 1821, for Caroline's cause died with her.

After the excitement of her case politics for the rest of Lord Liverpool's administration were an anticlimax. The years of distress which had done so much to keep the political temperature high came to an end, with economic recovery marking most of the 1820s. The ministry, renowned for repression in the post-war years of adversity, responded to the new climate by relaxing its authoritarian stance. So

15 The trial of Queen Caroline, 1820

marked was the change that it has been seen as a transition to so-called liberal toryism. The 'liberal Tories' included George Canning, who became foreign secretary in 1822 following Castlereagh's suicide, and Robert Peel who as home secretary presided over many reforms including the establishment of the metropolitan police force. Their policies left little room for the Whigs to complain. As Lord Grey admitted in 1824, 'there is no public question which excites, no public feeling which produces any sympathy, no public prospects which can engage me in future speculations'.

Even the impetus for reform seemed to have relaxed. 'The prosperity of the country', claimed Lord Lansdowne in 1825, 'has driven reform almost out of the heads of the reformers.' This was something of an exaggeration. A few reform measures were raised even in this decade. In 1821 the notoriously corrupt Cornish borough of Grampound was disfranchised and its two seats allocated to Yorkshire, the first change in English constituencies since the reign of Charles II. In 1822 Lord Russell proposed to transfer some hundred borough seats to counties and unrepresented towns. Although he was defeated by 269 votes to 164 the minority was the largest vote in favour of reform since 1785.

In the last years of Liverpool's ministry the main division was between ultra-Tories on the right and liberal Tories and Whigs on the left. When the prime minister had a stroke in 1827, therefore, and resigned, Canning, leader of the liberal Tories, formed a government which included some Whigs. That summer, however, Canning died suddenly and one of his supporters, Lord Goderich, took over. Goderich presided over one of the shortest-lived ministries in British history, which could claim the distinction of never having to face parliament. On Goderich's resignation the king asked the Duke of Wellington to form a government.

The Wellington ministry marked a crucial stage in the development of party politics. Until Lord Liverpool's death the political situation had been one of a Tory party, as it was increasingly being called, in office, with widespread support in parliament and the country, and a Whig party in opposition prone to fragmentation at Westminster and appealing very little either to independent MPs or to the general public. In the years 1828 to 1830 all that changed. The Tory party fell apart, losing the support of the independents and of the electors, who went over to a united and confident Whig party.

The main reason for this rapid transition was that in 1829 Wellington felt constrained to carry Catholic emancipation by repealing the penal laws which deprived Catholics of full civil rights. Tories who felt that the constitution in church and state had already been jeopardised by the repeal of the Test and Corporation Acts the previous year regarded this as the last straw. The prime minister considered himself to have no alternative, since the election of a Catholic, Daniel O'Connell, for County Clare forced his hand. He could either get parliament to declare O'Connell unqualified to take his seat, and risk a repetition of the Wilkes episode in much more adverse circumstances, or he could give Catholics full civil rights including the vote. His ultra-Tory opponents argued that he should have got the king to dissolve parliament. Yet this would almost certainly have produced a majority opposed to emancipation.

Nothing reveals more clearly the conservatism of many electors and even unenfranchised subjects than the fact that there were 20,000 petitions against Catholic emancipation. Wellington paradoxically played into the hands of the reformers by revealing how out of touch the unreformed parliament was with the conservative rather than with the radical attitudes of the public. Even some ultra-Tories now accepted the notion that parliamentary reform was desirable. Thus the Marquis of Blandford proposed in February 1830 the abolition of all rotten boroughs, their seats to be transferred to counties and cities, a household franchise in boroughs and the extension of the vote to copyholders in the counties. Though this was comfortably defeated, a motion put by Russell that Birmingham, Leeds and Manchester should be given seats was only lost by a narrow margin.

Reform emerged as the great issue at the polls in 1830. A general election, made necessary by the death of George IV, and fought against a background of economic recession, indicated that the popular vote was committed to it. The results, however, did not indicate a clear majority for a reforming measure. Indeed the first Reform Bill was eventually defeated in the new House. Wellington even tried to continue in office after parliament met, but deserted by so many of his Tory allies, ultra as well as liberal, his manoeuvres were of no avail. He helped to precipitate his own downfall in a notorious speech opposing any kind of reform, claiming that 'the country possessed at the present moment a legislature which answered all the good purposes of legislation, and this to a greater degree than any legislature ever had answered in any country whatsoever. He would go further and say that the legislature and the system of representation possessed the full and entire confidence of the country.' His government actually fell in November on a motion about the civil list.

Earl Grey then formed a ministry pledged to reform. A committee chaired by Lord Durham proposed a scheme to the cabinet in January 1831 for the redistribution of seats and the extension of the franchise. Sixty-one boroughs were to lose both their seats, and forty-seven were to lose one. Most of these were to be allocated to counties and to large towns. There was to be a property qualification for borough voters of households valued at £20 a year. The new electors were to vote by secret ballot. This last proposal was dropped by the cabinet largely on the grounds that balloting was furtive and unworthy of Englishmen. They then reduced the household qualification to £10. A bill on this basis was consequently introduced into parliament by Lord John Russell in March. The second reading passed the Commons by a bare majority: 302 to 301. In April the bill was defeated in committee and Grey asked the king for a dissolution.

The general election of 1831 was fought over the single issue of reform. It resulted in a mandate for 'the bill, the whole bill and nothing but the bill'. Where over 200 independents had been returned in 1830, now there were just over 50. The pro-reform Whigs numbered 370, the anti-reform Tories 235. As a result the bill sailed through the lower House, obtaining a second reading by 367 votes to 231 and a final reading by 345 to 236. Then on 8 October it was defeated in the Lords. A third bill had to be introduced, in which some amendments were incorporated. Thus the number of boroughs to lose both seats was reduced to fifty-six while the number of those which were to lose one was lowered to thirty. This bill passed its third reading in March 1832 by 355 to 239. Yet although the Lords granted it a second reading it was defeated in a committee of the upper House on 7 May. Grey asked William IV to give him the strength to force it through the Lords by creating fifty new peers. When the king refused the prime minister resigned. Wellington tried to form a ministry but failed. William then had little choice but to turn to Grey again and promise to ennoble enough men to pass the bill if necessary. In June the bill obtained a third reading by 106 to 22. Clearly a great many peers chose to abstain

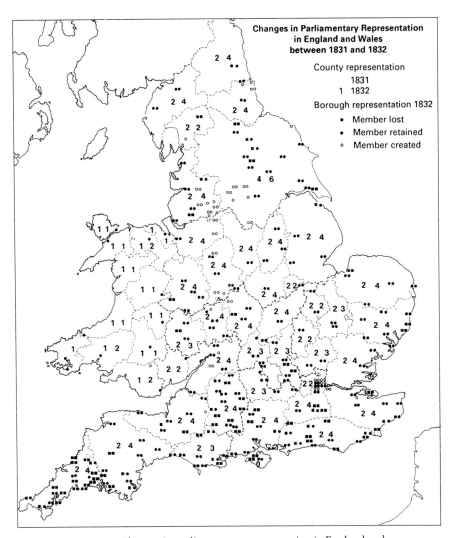

Map 2 Changes in parliamentary representation in England and Wales, 1831–2

rather than to give the king the embarrassment of packing the upper House. On 7 June William gave the bill the royal assent. He refused to attend in person and ordered that no public celebrations were to be held to mark the passing of the Reform Act.

The king clearly felt that he had been coerced. How far the bill had found its way on to the statute book by coercion is open to argument. Certainly there were attempts to put pressure on parliament to pass it. After the defeat of the first bill in October 1831 there were riots in Bristol, where the bishop's palace was looted, and Nottingham, where the castle was burned. When the Duke of Wellington tried to form a ministry in May 1832 there was considerable outside agitation against him. The Birmingham Political Union, a body established in 1830, was said to be pledged to lead an uprising in that city, and to have been promised 1,500 armed men. Francis Place, a leader of the London radicals, claimed to have been offered the services of a military leader, a mysterious Polish count. That such rumours frightened the victor of Waterloo into resigning his office, however, can be discounted.

Moreover, the majority for reform in the Commons were not motivated by fear but by conviction. They were convinced that the anomalies of the unreformed electoral system were indefensible and that some redistribution was necessary to bring the middle classes within the pale of the constitution. It was a concession based on an acceptance of the justice of their claims rather than a surrender extorted by threats. As Lord Macaulay put it, the principle behind the measure was 'to admit the middle class to a large and direct share in the representation'. He went on to claim that it achieved this 'without any violent shock to the institutions of our country', in contrast to the exaggerated prophesies of a minority who predicted that it upset the equilibrium of the Commons so much as to threaten the survival of the crown and the House of Lords.

The actual changes made by the act were more modest. The electorate in England and Wales was increased from an estimated 366,250 to 652,777 voters who were first registered under the new arrangements for electoral registration, an increase of 78 per cent. In Scotland the expansion was even more remarkable, from about 4,000 to 65,000, giving the Scottish electorate a genuine identity for the first time since the Act of Union. The change was felt most in the counties, where to the time-honoured forty-shilling freeholders were added £10 copyholders and £50 leaseholders. This boosted the shire electorates in England and Wales by 83 per cent. The counties also benefited from the redistribution of seats, Yorkshire obtaining a total of six, twenty-six others four, and seven three knights of the shire. Even then the ratio of county to borough seats remained adverse to the shires for a country still preponderantly rural. Twenty-two boroughs obtained representation and were given two seats, including Birmingham, Leeds, Manchester and Sheffield, while nineteen were given one, including Whitby. The principle of enfranchisement in the towns was based on households with a rateable value of £10 per annum. Since property values varied greatly from one region to another enormous anomalies were created. In London, where values were high, many households qualified, and the result was a significant increase in the electorate to enfranchise even skilled workers. In Leeds, by contrast, where values were low, few households qualified, with the result that only about 5,000 voters were registered in a city with 125,000 inhabitants. The new electorates thus created did not enfranchise the middle class in the sense of extending the vote to the emergent manufacturing interest. Rather the vote was granted to tradesmen such as had enjoyed the franchise in the old freemen boroughs. Yet the notion of representing interests rather than individuals was used to justify such anomalies. Thus Whitby was given the vote, and not Doncaster, a town of similar size, on the grounds that the port represented the fishing interest.

The outcome was that two broad types of constituency emerged. There were rural constituencies, counties and market towns, which retained many features of the traditional electoral system, and there were the cities given seats for the first time. Some of these quickly acquired familiar characteristics. Huddersfield, for example, came under the sway of the Ramsdens, a prosperous mill-owning family. But others displayed a decided independence, being frequently contested and experiencing high turn-outs.

The survival of types of electoral behaviour from the unreformed into the reformed era owed much to the endurance of deference communities in rural areas well into the nineteenth century. The aristocracy and gentry continued to hold sway in the counties and market towns. Some boroughs even remained proprietary after 1832, for instance Ripon. The survival of such constituencies has been attributed to a deliberate design on the part of some supporters of the Reform Act, who conceded seats to the new manufacturing interests on the understanding that they would be entitled to unchallenged rule in their own bailiwicks. Thus a clause in the original bill which prevented forty-shilling freeholders in boroughs from polling in counties, and the so-called Chandos clause which enfranchised £50 tenants, have both been attributed to a rearguard action by country gentlemen anxious to cure the developments which had made reform appear essential rather than to concede electoral influence to them. While in fact it appears to have happened more by chance than by design the continuities in many rural constituencies from before 1832 did ensure that reform did not mean an abrupt change of the whole system.

Although the electoral system had not been adjusted to give power to the middle classes, it nevertheless was intended to cater for their interests. These found expression in further reforms, such as the abolition of slavery in the British Empire in 1833; the Poor Law Amendment Act of 1834; and the Municipal Corporations Act of 1835.

The abolition of slavery was the successful culmination of a campaign which had united humanitarians of all parties. Its leading advocate for decades had been Pitt's old ally William Wilberforce, an evangelical Tory. Although taken up by many Whig candidates at the general election of 1832 it did not divide the new parliament along party lines. Even so the Reform Act materially assisted its passage, since the enlarged constituencies returned over a hundred MPs pledged to support repeal, while the disfranchisement of several small boroughs deprived the slavery lobby of some supporters. They were still powerful enough to negotiate £20,000,000 from the government by way of compensation for their 'losses'.

The Poor Law Amendment Act, though it was to raise violent opposition outside parliament, received very little inside. At most fifty members raised objections, some radicals, some Tories and some Irish. The bulk of MPs of all parties supported a measure which they felt had the overwhelming approval of the newly enfranchised classes. It took poor relief out of the hands of the justices of the peace and parish officials who had previously administered it and made it the responsibility of boards of guardians, elected to supervise unions of parishes and responsible to central poor law commissioners. The principle of less eligibility whereby recipients of poor relief were to be less well off than the earners of the poorest wages lay behind the new scheme. By its supporters it was defended as ensuring that paupers had incentives to seek employment and to become self-sufficient. By its opponents it was castigated as an excuse to reduce the costs of relieving the poor. One way of realising the principle was to insist on the abolition of outdoor relief and the provision of indoor relief in union workhouses where the sexes were separated. These provisions aroused bitter resentment. The act was regarded as evidence that the vote did give electors access to the machinery of legislation which could be used to enact measures in the interests of the enfranchised and to the detriment of non-voters. It did more than any other enactment of the reformed parliament to persuade many of the unenfranchised that the vote was vital to protect their interests.

The Municipal Corporations Act replaced the self-perpetuating oligarchies of 179 borough corporations with elected councillors chosen by householders who paid rates, a more extensive franchise than that of the Reform Act, which even included women ratepayers. It gave the urban middle classes a direct say in the government of their cities and towns. The act had a fairly easy passage through parliament even though many of the ancient corporations it replaced were Tory strongholds, while the newly constituted municipalities fell into Whig hands from the start. The royal commission which investigated the boroughs, while it produced a voluminous report, had made up its mind that they were corrupt and unjustifiable anachronisms even before the inquiry commenced. The resultant statute was not therefore a Whig measure.

By contrast religious issues continued to divide Whigs and Tories during the 1830s. The Reform Act of 1832 brought to an end the long era in which the established church had enjoyed preferential treatment from the state. Public money ceased to be voted for the building of new churches. The Whigs adopted an attitude which has been dubbed 'liberal Anglicanism' towards such issues as giving surplus revenues from the Church of Ireland to secular charities and to treating nonconformist schools on a par with Anglican education establishments as recipients of state subsidies. This attitude did much to aid the recovery of the Tory party during the 1830s. In 1832 the Tories were reduced to 150 MPs. In 1835 they obtained 290 seats; in 1837,

313; and finally at the general election of 1841 they gained a majority. Sir Robert Peel took office, the first prime minister to do so directly as a result of winning an election.

Religion remained central to politics under Peel. Thus in 1845 his proposal to increase the government grant to the Catholic college at Maynooth in Ireland aroused considerable opposition. Petitions poured in against it. Where in the 1830s, however, religious issues had polarised the parties, the Maynooth grant split them. Gladstone resigned from the ministry over it. Tories divided almost evenly for and against it and Peel only got it through with Whig support. This was a harbinger of the disintegration of the Tory party over the repeal of the Corn Laws.

The Corn Laws, the first of which was passed in 1815, laid protective duties on imported wheat and other cereals. Opponents of the scheme objected that this protected the producers of staple food at the expense of the consumers. Led by John Bright and Richard Cobden they protested that this was a paradigm case of the abuse of its privileges by the landed elite. In 1838 they founded the Anti-Corn Law League in Manchester to campaign for repeal. The League lambasted landowners and raised the cry of 'cheap bread' in the general election of 1841. It went on to field candidates at by-elections, though it quickly learned that its prospects were better in manufacturing than in market towns. When the potato famine devastated Ireland in 1845 the League argued that grain should be shipped there at public expense to relieve the starvation. It also pointed out that to subsidise both Irish consumers and English producers was indefensible.

Peel arrived at the same conclusion independently. Indeed his budget strategy immediately after winning the election in 1841 was to reduce duties in the interests of free trade, making up the loss to the exchequer with a renewed income tax. He hoped to educate the Tory party gradually into accepting this fiscal policy to the point of dropping the tariffs on imported corn. The Irish famine left no time for a slow process of conversion. Instead he decided to repeal the Corn Laws immediately.

Peel's decision split the Tory party. Repeal divided Protectionists from Peelites. Although there was nothing to distinguish the MPs in the two camps socially, since most Tories were country gentlemen, there was a distinction between the types of constituencies which they represented. Protectionists sat for counties and market towns, while Peelites represented more the cities and manufacturing districts. This led Protectionists to claim that the landed interest had been defeated by the new interests enfranchised by the Reform Act, and even to blame the Anti-Corn Law League for the repeal. In fact, although the League was quite willing to accept responsibility, the repeal of the Corn Laws had no more to do with its agitation than the removal of Cruise missiles from British soil had to do with the Campaign for Nuclear Disarmament. Both were achieved because of executive decisions taken by governments impervious to the pressure groups.

Where the agitation against the Corn Laws can be seen as the last great clash of interests in the eighteenth-century sense, the challenge presented by Chartism is generally regarded as the first clash in the class warfare of modern Britain. The proponents of the People's Charter saw the Reform Act as buying off the middle classes by giving them the vote. In their view the middle class used their electoral power to maintain their interests at the expense of the working class. The Poor Law Amendment Act of 1834 was a direct consequence of reform and seemed to be designed to ease the cost of relieving poverty which fell largely on the middle classes by increasing the difficulty of obtaining relief on the part of the workers. In order to protect working-class interests, therefore, the obtaining of the vote for all adult males was essential.

What aroused working-class consciousness even more than the poor law was the Dorchester labourers' case. In 1834 six members of the Friendly Society of Agricultural Labourers, better known as the Tolpuddle martyrs, were sentenced to seven years transportation to Australia for joining an illegal combination, the illegality being the technical one that they had administered secret oaths. William Lovett, a London joiner, established the Dorchester Committee to organise protests against the sentences. In 1836 Lovett became the co-founder, along with Henry Hetherington, of the London Working Men's Association. Two years later this body sponsored the National Charter to demand universal manhood suffrage, annual parliaments, the secret ballot, equal electoral districts, the payment of MPs and the abolition of property qualifications for entry into the House of Commons. Chartism was born.

The Charter, with its six points, was presented to parliament three

16   The Kennington Common meeting of Chartists, 10 April
1848

times: in July 1839; again in May 1842; and finally in April 1848. On
the first occasion the accompanying petition was alleged to contain
4,300,000 signatures, on the second 3,300,000 and on the third
5,700,000. The third petition was examined with suspicious rapidity by
a Commons committee, which claimed that it contained fewer than
2,000,000 names, including such bogus ones as Mr Punch and Queen
Victoria. Even this surely very conservative estimate nevertheless
reveals that Chartism did have genuine mass support.

Sustaining this support, and channelling it into a political movement,
presented Chartist leaders with a formidable problem. The leadership
was divided anyway, particularly between the capital and the provinces. Although the lead was taken by London the agitation quickly
spread, particularly in manufacturing and mining districts. In the north
of England the Methodist J. R. Stephens and Feargus O'Connor,
editor of the *Northern Star* could command huge followings.
O'Connor, indeed, was not initially the megalomaniac he later became,
but on the contrary was a charismatic figure whose influence on the
movement was greater than that of other aspirants to its leadership.
The diffuse leadership was to some extent a reflection of the divergent

aims of different Chartists. Some, especially the Londoners, urged moral persuasion by peaceful petitioning. Others advocated physical force, and there actually was an armed uprising in Newport, Monmouthshire, in 1839.

The rising occurred during the depression of 1837 to 1839. Many historians have seen the ebb and flow of Chartism as a gut reaction to economic conditions, echoing Stephens's words that it was 'a knife and fork question'. However, the depression did not affect the north-east of England or the south-west of Scotland to any great extent. Yet Newcastle upon Tyne and Glasgow became important regional centres of the Chartist movement. Moreover the Charter was not demanding the dole but parliamentary representation for the working class. The achievement of the vote was intended to gain for workers a recognition of their interests such as the Reform Act had acquired for the middle class. Those interests were badly affected by economic recession, and it is not therefore surprising that Chartism did have more support in a slump than when the economy recovered.

Not that those in power ignored the interests of the working classes completely. Although they steadfastly refused to accept the Charter, showing once again that the ruling class rather closed ranks when under threat, nevertheless some concessions to working-class agitation were made. Amongst them the most important was the Ten Hours Act of 1847. This was the culmination of a campaign sustained for over a decade by Chartists, evangelical Tories such as Lord Ashley and Richard Oastler, and radical reformers like John Fielden of Todmorden. Of its successful passage Karl Marx was moved to observe that for the first time 'the political economy of the middle class succumbed to the political economy of the working class'.

The Chartist agitation played little part, however, in the general election of 1847, which was dominated by the issues arising out of religion and repeal of the Corn Laws. The divided Tories were swept aside at the polls, and indeed found themselves in the minority at every general election until 1874, which took place after the passing of the second Reform Act. It is true that there were Conservative ministries led by Lord Derby in 1852, 1858 and 1866, but these were minority governments which did not have the support of the electorate. Some Peelites joined the first after the death of Peel himself in 1850 and Derby's abandonment of protection. Most, however, supported Lord

Aberdeen's coalition government in 1852, which laid the basis for the development of the Liberal party.

Derby's first ministry was formed after Lord John Russell, who succeeded Peel as prime minister in 1846, lost the support of the Irish members at Westminster. Russell forfeited their normal sympathy for the Whigs with an outburst against 'papal aggression'. When the Pope restored the Catholic hierarchy in 1850, giving the leader of the Catholic clergy in England the title of Archbishop of Westminster, Russell, either impetuously or with a calculated opportunism which backfired, published a condemnation of this appointment and followed it up with a bill to prevent Catholic bishops from holding English titles. Although the bill passed, it alienated the Irish who took the first opportunity to bring the Whigs down. The Conservatives, however, found it hard to construct a ministry to replace Russell's. Derby's minority government earned notoriety as the 'Who? who?' ministry because of the deaf Duke of Wellington's audible incredulity at hearing a list of its ministers read out in the House of Lords. It lasted until December 1852, when it was defeated after the first of the classic encounters between Benjamin Disraeli and William Gladstone. Disraeli as chancellor of the exchequer introduced a budget, the principal feature of which was a distinction between earned and unearned income for tax purposes. At one o'clock in the morning Gladstone demolished its premises with a brilliant speech. He subsequently accepted the office of chancellor in Lord Aberdeen's administration.

Aberdeen presided over a coalition of Peelites like himself and Gladstone, and Whigs such as Lord John Russell and Palmerston, veterans of the Grey ministry which had passed the Reform Act. It was a peacetime reforming administration unfortunately overtaken by the Crimean War. Thus Gladstone's budget of 1853 was posited on the phasing out of income tax, a proposition set aside by the financial requirements of the war effort. Similarly Russell's Reform Bill of 1854, which aimed at extending and deepening the franchise, was abandoned after the outbreak of the war.

Russian expansion into the Balkans at Turkey's expense was seen as a threat to the balance of power. Aberdeen was, however, reluctant to support Turkey, since he regarded it as a corrupt Islamic tyranny which persecuted Christian minorities within its domains. The 'hawks' in his cabinet, led by Palmerston, overcame his reluctance. They were assisted by a vociferous press campaign. Such papers as the *Daily Telegraph*, *Morning Chronicle* and *Morning Herald* exploited a belligerent nationalism which bayed for war against Russia.

When war broke out in 1854 the British army was exposed to investigative journalism which made the newspaper-reading public at home – and unfortunately abroad – more aware of conflict than ever before. At first the campaign to take Sebastopol from the Russians went reasonably well, with victories at Alma and Inkerman. As the port failed to fall before the harsh winter of 1854–5, however, requiring the British to dig in until the spring, the inadequacies of their military and naval capacity to sustain the siege were exposed, especially in the dispatches of the correspondent for *The Times*. Aberdeen's government could not survive the glare of publicity and was brought down on a motion to set up a parliamentary committee to investigate its conduct of the war.

Palmerston was the inevitable choice of prime minister, though the queen tried to avoid it. He constructed a coalition cabinet on lines similar to those of Aberdeen's. Despite prominent Peelites, including Gladstone, leaving it soon after, his government survived. Palmerston was helped by a turn for the better in the Crimea. Sebastopol finally fell to its British and French besiegers in 1855, while the army fared much better through the winter of 1855–6 than it had done the previous year. The prime minister was even able to present the Peace of Paris, which ended the war in 1856, as a triumph. Although it was criticised at the time and since, it neutralised the Black Sea as a zone for naval combat which was a not insignificant outcome of the hostilities.

The Crimean War boosted Palmerston's belligerent image. He projected it further with wars in Persia and China. His aggressive foreign policy led to a debate on a motion of no confidence in which Disraeli challenged him to go to the country on the election slogan 'No Reform! New Taxes! Canton blazing! Persia invaded!' When the motion was carried Palmerston did indeed get the queen to dissolve parliament and won the subsequent general election. The 1857 elections are generally regarded as a victory for Palmerstonian politics. Certainly his radical opponents were routed, both Bright and Cobden losing their seats. But Palmerston could scarcely complain that the majority owed him personal favours when it turned against him in 1858. After an attempt on the life of the French emperor, Louis Napoleon protested that the assassination plot had been hatched in Britain and demanded measures against terrorists there. Palmerston responded by agreeing to suppress foreign terrorists residing on British soil and brought in a Conspiracy to Murder Bill. The bill backfired, however, as truckling to a foreign power, and Palmerston resigned when it was defeated in parliament.

Lord Derby then formed another minority government. It was kept in power for over a year largely by the disarray of its opponents, who formed a motley array of Liberals, Peelites, radicals and Whigs. Derby tried to tempt the leading Peelite, Gladstone, to join his government. Had he succeeded the history of later Victorian politics might have been very different. Gladstone refused, however, because, as he put it, 'the reconstitution of a party can only be effected, if at all, by the return of the old influences to their places and not by the junction of an isolated person'.

Parties were in fact in a state of flux during the 1850s. The Conservatives under Derby abandoned protection, removed the requirement for MPs to be possessed of property real or personal, and committed themselves to a measure of parliamentary reform. Indeed with these developments the party really lost its previous identity and even any ideological reason for its existence. It is a tribute to the political skills and loyalties of Derby and especially of his ablest lieutenant Benjamin Disraeli that they kept it together through a generation in the wilderness, or at least in an apparently permanent minority.

Reform indeed occasioned the fall of this government. Russell proposed a more radical measure, resulting in a ministerial defeat in parliament. Derby decided not simply to resign but to go to the country. Although the results of the 1859 election were a distinct improvement on those of 1857 for the prime minister's supporters it still left their rivals in the majority. In response to the prospect of another Conservative minority government kept in power by their own disarray its opponents came together at a historic meeting in Willis's rooms in June 1859 which has since been generally seen as the birth of the modern Liberal party.

Shortly after the meeting the united opposition brought down the Derby government on a straight vote of no confidence. This was the fifth time that a ministry had been effectively dismissed by a majority in the Commons since 1852. The 1850s thus constituted a unique decade in British political history, marked by what contemporaries termed 'parliamentary government'. In the previous century majorities had been held together by the influence of the executive. The decline of the crown's ability to sustain support for ministries had to some extent been superseded by the rise of party in the early nineteenth century. But the collapse of the Tory party in 1846 ushered in an era when the independent member enjoyed more power to make or break ministries than at any time before or since. It was to prove a brief interlude. After 1859 party discipline was to exert sufficient control over proceedings in the Commons to replace parliamentary with party government.

Indeed the Liberal party foisted Palmerston on to Victoria as prime minister after Derby's defeat. The Queen preferred Lord Granville as her principal adviser, but he failed to form a government.

Palmerston's last ministry was dominated by foreign affairs to an unusual degree, domestic concerns being by comparison uneventful. The prime minister boasted in 1864 that 'there is really nothing to be done. We cannot go on adding to the Statute Book *ad infinitum*.' This was probably said in jest, and was an underestimation of his own achievement. His government presided over the Bankruptcy Act of 1861, the Companies Act of 1862 and a Poor Law Act of 1864 which effectively ended settlement, that is, the need for claimants to establish that they were 'settled' in the parish where they claimed relief. Palmerston probably played down domestic issues, all too aware that they could shatter the new-found unity of the Liberals. He was relieved when Russell abandoned his reform bill as the price of becoming foreign secretary. Palmerston pursued a vigorous foreign policy, perhaps on the grounds that playing a prominent role on the world stage would appeal to the electorate and thus insure him against a parliamentary defeat.

The most prominent feature on the international scene when the ministry was formed was Italy. The movement for Italian unification reached its peak in the years 1859 to 1861. In 1859 the peninsula consisted of seven separate territories. Two years later it was unified under the crown of Piedmont-Savoy, only the territories controlled by the Pope in Rome and the Austrians in Venice remaining outside the new kingdom. Britain's role was that of an interested but not involved power. Some cabinet ministers, including Palmerston himself, Gladstone, who was chancellor of the exchequer, and Russell were sympathetic to Italian aspirations. Others, however, were wary of the way these took the form of antagonism towards Austrian influence in northern Italy. These were encouraged by the queen and Prince Albert, who did not sympathise with the liberal aspects of Italian nationalism. At the same time all British politicians were suspicious of French ambitions south of the Alps. Although these years witnessed a *rapprochement* between Britain and France, signalised by the commercial treaty of 1860, Louis Napoleon's alignment with Piedmont against Austria was regarded with suspicion, especially when it obtained for him the annexation of Nice and Savoy. There was relief in Britain when the French emperor abandoned Piedmont and did a deal with Austria. Now that Italian nationalism was unsullied by French imperialism it could be cheered from the sidelines. Garibaldi's success in bringing Naples and Sicily within the new nation was welcomed by the cabinet.

As Italy was coming together, the United States of America were falling apart. The start of the American Civil War in 1861 posed opportunities and problems for the British government. Some politicians welcomed the secession of the Confederacy because it created a balance of power in North America which they thought would be in Britain's interest. Others were even sympathetic to the South, preferring its aristocratic ethos to the bourgeois image of the North. Problems arose through the dependence of the Lancashire cotton mills on the supply of their raw material from the southern states. When these were cut off the resultant cotton famine created unemployment and hardship in the north-west of England. According to John Bright these influences divided society along class lines, the aristocracy and its bourgeois clients supporting the South while the unenfranchised workers upheld the North.

Although many historians have echoed this assertion the truth was more complicated. The 'Trent' affair, in which two southern agents *en route* to England were arrested by a northern official off Cuba, provoked tension between President Lincoln and Palmerston. Yet it was Prince Albert who cooled down the belligerents in the cabinet, rendering his last service to his adopted country before his death. And it was the aristocrats Lords Palmerston and Russell who reprimanded

Gladstone after a speech in Newcastle upon Tyne in which he virtually recognised the sovereignty of the Confederacy.

If the rulers of Britain were very much divided on the issue so were British subjects, the mill operatives of Lancashire being far from united in support of the North. On the contrary, as Mary Ellison has demonstrated, Bright did not speak for them. Many workers in the cotton mills actually favoured the southern cause. The degree of commitment varied throughout Lancashire not according to differences of politics or religion but directly depending upon the intensity of the unemployment caused by the cotton famine. Politicians were deceived because the unemployed workers did not actually riot or demonstrate violently. Those who recalled the Chartist disturbances associated physical-force Chartism with depressed areas. They were relieved when a depression in the cotton textile districts did not produce a resurgence of working-class militancy. To some extent this was attributable to more effective poor relief. But it was attributed to sympathy with the war aims of the Unionists. It had lasting effects on politics. In the debates on the Reform Bill of 1866 Robert Lowe expressed a contemptuous view of the working class. 'If you want venality,' he asked, 'if you want drunkenness and facility for being intimidated...if...you want impulsive, unreflecting and violent people...do you go to the top or the bottom?' Gladstone answered with the single word 'Lancashire.'

In the case of Italy and even of America Britain's naval strength earned her respect as a great power, but where military resources counted she could not exert the same influence, as the Crimean War had shown. The dispute between Denmark and Prussia over the duchies of Schleswig and Holstein was to demonstrate this again. Palmerston blustered about helping the Danes, but his bluff was exposed in 1864 when Bismarck annexed the duchies on behalf of Prussia and Austria. The Tories forthwith introduced a motion of censure in both houses of parliament, claiming that the government's failure 'to maintain their avowed policy of upholding the integrity and independence of Denmark...has lowered the just influence of this country in the counsels of Europe, and thereby diminished the securities for peace'. It was carried by nine votes in the Lords but in the Commons, after a debate lasting four days, it was lost when an amendment supported by the government was carried by 313 votes to

295. Even Disraeli, the mover of the motion, could not suppress his admiration for Palmerston who 'after the division scrambled up a wearing staircase to the ladies' gallery ... What pluck! To mount those dreadful stairs at three o'clock in the morning and eighty years of age.'

Palmerston lived to fight another general election held, in Lord Stanley's words, 'on no particular issue except confidence in the prime minister'. He won. In July 1865, 370 Liberals were returned and 288 Conservatives. Three months later 'Pam' was dead.

5

From the second Reform Act to the Boer War

On Palmerston's death Lord Russell formed a government committed to parliamentary reform, an issue which his predecessor had put on ice for the past five years. The difficulties the new prime minister would face from his own party had been demonstrated in 1865 when a private member's bill had been defeated by a combination of Tories and anti-reform Liberals. The latter formed the nucleus of what John Bright was to dub the 'Cave of Adullam' from the biblical hiding-place where David gathered around him 'everybody that was in distress, and everyone that was in debt, and everyone that was discontented'. The Adullamites combined with the Conservatives to defeat Russell's bill. He thereupon resigned, to be replaced by Lord Derby, who once again formed a minority government. Derby announced that he 'did not intend a third time to be made a mere stop gap until it should suit the convenience of the Liberal party to forget their dissensions and bring forward a measure which should oust us from office and replace them there'. He proposed to keep the Liberals divided and to sustain his own ministry in office by passing a measure of reform. He was fortified in this resolve by the support of the monarch, whose views he treated with as much deference as any Victorian politician. Besides, as he told Disraeli, 'The queen wants "us" to settle it.'

Victoria looked to the Conservatives to settle the question of reform presumably anticipating that a measure passed by them would be less radical than any enacted by their rivals. In the event, however, the second Reform Act when it became law was more sweeping in its scope than anybody could have expected. It enfranchised all male householders in boroughs who had been resident a year and had personally paid their rates. It even gave the vote to lodgers who paid at least £10 a year in rent. In the counties it lowered the property qualification to £12 per annum. The effect of these changes was to increase the electorate in England and Wales from 965,000 to 1,997,000. The increase was more marked in the boroughs, whose electorates grew by 134 per cent between 1866 and 1869, than in the counties, which increased by 37 per cent. In Scotland the number of voters in burghs nearly tripled, from some 55,000 to 152,000. A separate Scottish Reform Act passed the following year redistributed seven English seats disfranchised in 1867, three to counties, two to universities, one to Dundee and one to Glasgow. Altogether English boroughs lost fifty-two seats in the redistribution of the second Reform Act, twenty-three of which were added to the counties.

Liberals claimed that the addition of seats to the shires was a partisan measure to strengthen the Tory interest.

Certainly Disraeli had in mind his party's advantage throughout the manoeuvrings on the bill. But however much he might have wished to gerrymander constituencies he could not drive through a blatantly partisan measure since the ministry lacked a majority in the Commons. For the bill to survive he had to exploit the divisions among his opponents and retain some of them on his side. At first he picked up some Adullamite supporters, who thought that the Conservative bill was bound to be more restrictive than Russell's had been, and grudgingly accepted that reform was irresistible now that both parties had espoused it. Yet this tactic failed. Adullamites refused to join the ministry, while some Tory ministers, also opposed to reform, resigned. Disraeli demonstrated that he was a master tactician when, in order to retain control of the Commons, he then appealed to the radicals in the Liberal ranks. The bill consequently became progressively more radical. A residential ratepaying qualification was initially offset by proposals to balance the extension of the franchise thus created by giving more weight to wealthier voters, for instance by allowing certain categories two votes. These proposals were abandoned. Eventually the safeguard that resident householders should pay their own rates was substantially undermined by an amendment abolishing compound ratepaying, whereby rates were included in the rent and paid by the landlord. In parliamentary boroughs rates had to be deducted from the rent and paid by the tenant. It has been estimated that this amendment alone enabled over 400,000 compound ratepayers to qualify, and eventually added almost a million householders in England and Wales to the electoral register.

The acceptance of Hodgkinson's amendment, as it was known, has been attributed to outside pressure. Certainly there was agitation for reform, notably from two organisations; the Reform League and the Reform Union. Both organised meetings to keep up the pressure for reform from the collapse of Russell's ministry to the meeting of parliament following the formation of Derby's. The Union's membership tended to be middle class and therefore, in Victorian eyes, 'respectable'. The League, however, held mass rallies, such as those in Hyde Park of July 1866 and May 1867. The fact that Hodgkinson's amendment was accepted shortly after the second rally has been seen by some as more than a mere coincidence, and much stress has been placed on Disraeli's admission that he accepted it 'to destroy the present agitation and extinguish Gladstone and Co.' The phrase 'the present agitation', however, almost certainly refers to radical demands for reform inside rather than outside parliament. Disraeli needed the support of parliamentary radicals to sustain his majority in the Commons. Had he given way to extra-parliamentary pressure he would have lost the support of Conservatives in his own ranks.

Not that consideration of the world beyond Whitehall was totally lacking in Disraeli's calculations. Quite the reverse; the social implications of reform were crucial to them. Since the demise of Chartism and the rise of the so-called 'labour aristocracy' in the years after 1848, the case for extending the franchise to include the 'respectable' elements in the working class among the electorate had impressed itself on both parties. They distinguished the artisanate from the 'residuum', the 'rowdies' and 'roughs' at the bottom of the social heap. They sought to enfranchise respectable artisans while leaving the 'residuum' voteless. The problem was how to make a statutory distinction between them. Russell and Gladstone had first tried in 1866 to draw a dividing line using the rateable values of households, but had eventually abandoned this as being technically too complex and sought instead to establish a division based on rents. Disraeli disliked the rental distinction partly because he was led to believe that it would only produce a minor extension of the franchise to the better-off artisans and that would benefit the Liberals. He put forward more radical proposals in 1867 not simply for tactical purposes but also because he genuinely believed that the more artisans were enfranchised the better that would be for the Conservative party. Hence his insistence on the personal payment of rates, which he maintained was a sure sign of respectability. Hence also Gladstone's attempt to amend it by proposing a minimum rateable value rather than the enfranchisement of all ratepayers. It was a bit disingenuous of 'the People's William' to assert this as a counter-principle to Disraeli's when he himself had abandoned it as impractical the previous year. Such partisan considerations helped to precipitate the 'tea room revolt' on the part of Liberals who refused to support Gladstone's restrictive amendment, thereby ensuring its defeat. Many MPs, however, were anxious about the effects of a household franchise, worried in case it swamped some constituencies with working-class voters. They were the more perturbed when a report commissioned in 1865 revealed that substantially more working men had been enfranchised in many boroughs by the first Reform Act than had been envisaged by its framers.

The Conservative solution to this problem was to try to insulate the counties and market towns from the new industrial conurbations. To some extent they succeeded. As we have seen the franchise in the counties was expanded much less drastically than in the boroughs. Moreover the redistribution of seats still left the rural areas with more representatives than they should have had given the fact that more people lived in towns than in the countryside, as the 1851 census had revealed. This created such anomalies that, unlike the first Reform Act, the second was not regarded as a 'final' solution to the problem of representation. It was widely accepted that further redistribution, if not extension of the franchise, was inevitable.

The passing of the second Reform Act marked a transition from a period of parliamentary government to one of party rule. Where after 1832 ministries had changed more as a result of defeats in parliament than at the polls, after 1867 they resigned as a result of general elections. Disraeli was the first to leave office, having replaced Derby as prime minister early in 1868. Although he was defeated by the opposition in May, he held out until the autumn when an election could take place on the basis of the registers drawn up under the new provisions.

The Liberals were able to defeat Disraeli because they had found an issue on which they could unite after the disarray into which they had been thrown by the question of reform. The issue round which they rallied was the disestablishment of the Church of Ireland, the Irish branch of the Anglican community which, though it catered to only a fifth of the population, still had the status of an established church. Gladstone, whose belief in the ripeness of time had previously led him to postpone promoting the issue, now suddenly found that time was ripe for it. He had a knack of placing questions in a political hothouse if their 'ripeness' became expedient. The disestablishment of the Irish church thus formed a principal plank in the platform of the Liberal party in the 1868 elections. It brought together a curious alliance of Roman Catholics and Protestant nonconformists against the Church of Ireland. The high church Anglican Gladstone was even accused of being a crypto-Catholic on the hustings. He nevertheless obtained a mandate for the measure, with the Liberals obtaining 387 seats to the Conservatives 271.

Although the unity of the Liberals on the issue succeeded in carrying the disestablishment of the Church of Ireland, other Irish issues led once more to their fragmentation. Gladstone's famous utterance, 'My mission is to pacify Ireland', led some even of his own supporters to accuse him of appeasing the violence perpetrated by the Irish Republican Brotherhood, or Fenians as they were called. Their activities included such 'outrages' as an attack on a Manchester police station and a fatal explosion at Clerkenwell prison in 1867. One of the grievances which they exploited and which Gladstone hoped to remove was that of tenant-right, the customary claim, unrecognised by law, to retain, bequeath or even sell the occupancy of a holding. The problem was exacerbated by the fact that many tenants were Catholics and many landlords were Protestants and even absentees resident in England. But religious and ethnic differences did not cause the disputes. At bottom it was a disagreement over the nature of property. To landlords, especially those with English properties also, their proprietorship was absolute, backed by common and statute law. To their Catholic tenants immemorial custom gave those who mingled their labour with the soil a joint proprietorship in it. Gladstone's Land Act of 1870 made a timid attempt to reconcile these divergent views but satisfied neither, and indeed alienated many English landowners including some Whigs who traditionally supported the Liberals, because it was seen by them as an attack on property.

Finally an attempt to provide university education for all sects in Ireland, Catholics as well as Protestants, brought about the defeat of the government. Instead of endowing a separate Catholic University, Gladstone sought to merge Trinity College, Dublin and the Queen's Colleges founded by Peel in Belfast, Cork and Galway into one Irish institution. Some radicals objected to the bill's provisions aimed at avoiding inter-denominational confrontation, for instance by not appointing dons to teach religion, modern history or philosophy. Disraeli saw his chance and in the early hours of 12 March 1873 mustered a majority of three against the bill. Gladstone offered his resignation, but was confounded when Disraeli declined to form a government. The Tory leader refused to preside over a minority ministry, and was reluctant to risk a general election in 1873 since, although by-elections were going in favour of opposition candidates, the Liberals still looked like winning. So the Liberals limped on as a lame duck government until the general election of 1874, when the Conservatives won over 100 seats more than their rivals.

The Liberal defeat in 1874 is usually put down to their universal unpopularity with the electorate. As G. M. Young put it, 'In its six years of office this great but unfortunate administration contrived to offend, to disquiet, or to disappoint, almost every interest in the country.' What he termed the 'gentlemanly interest' was offended by the introduction of competitive examinations for entry into the civil service and the abolition of the purchase of commissions in the army. Anglicans were not only aghast at the disestablishment of the Church of Ireland but mortified by the final removal of religious tests at Oxford and Cambridge. Nor were the dissenters altogether pleased with the Education Act of 1870, introduced by W. E. Forster, the radical vice-president of the committee of Council for Education.

Forster's Education Act marked a major departure from the Liberal principle of non-intervention. As far as education was concerned they had long advocated voluntarism, but, although some influential Liberals continued to uphold the voluntary principle, most admitted by the late 1860s that it had not provided an adequate educational system. Some form of state provision was essential. The question was what form it should take. The National Education League, founded in 1869, wanted compulsory, free and non-sectarian schooling. Since most voluntary schools were Church of England establishments Anglicans responded by forming the National Education Union to advocate that the state should supplement the denominational schools. The 1870 Act was much more in line with the Union's proposals than with the League's. It authorised the setting up of school boards to inspect local educational provision and to establish board schools if it was deemed to be inadequate. Non-denominational religious instruction was to be provided in them, though parents could withdraw their children from such lessons if they objected.

Finally the Liberal government alienated the brewing and distilling interests with measures to restrict the sale of alcohol. A bill of 1871 which sought to regulate the issuing of licences roused the wrath of the whole drink trade before it was dropped. An act of 1872 limited the opening hours of licensed premises. Gladstone later attributed his party's defeat at the polls to the uproar created by these proposals. As he put it in a letter to his brother, 'We have been borne down in a torrent of gin and beer.'

This was the first general election at which such conclusions cannot be tested against the evidence of poll books. The Secret Ballot Act of 1872 put an end to the recording of votes cast at parliamentary elections. The introduction of the secret ballot, after decades of agitation for it, came about largely because of the corrupt practices at the general election of 1868, the first held under the extended franchise of the second Reform Act. Bribery was still blatant in some boroughs. In Beverley, for example, the novelist Anthony Trollope was defeated by a Tory machine so corrupt that his petition against it resulted in the town's disfranchisement. The secret ballot was held to be the only remedy against such practices. It did not come about through pressure from the constituencies. Nor can it be seriously attributed to pressure from electoral patrons who felt that their control over deference communities was being jeopardised by the expansion of the electorate. Rather it was introduced because of the conviction of leading politicians that it had become essential. Thus Gladstone, who had previously opposed it in true Victorian style on the grounds that it was 'unmanly', came round to the conclusion that it was a necessary safeguard against undue influence, whether of landlords, mill-owners or trade unions.

Gladstone actually analysed the outcome of the 1874 election in a published article. Some Liberals protested that they had been cheated of victory since they polled 1,263,254 votes against 1,071,325 cast for the Conservatives. Gladstone denied this, however, pointing out that there were too many uncontested constituencies, especially in safe Tory seats, for the totals to be meaningful, even though it was the first election at which both parties received more than a million votes. He put it down to the tendency of Whigs, Liberals and radicals to fight each other, leaving a clear field for their Conservative opponents. Modern psephologists offer a more sophisticated analysis, indicating a 5 per cent 'swing' to the Conservatives over the Liberals between 1868 and 1874. But the geographical variations show that local factors were still important. They also reveal that the Liberals held a majority of Scottish and Welsh seats and were strong in the north of England. Conservative successes were mainly in the counties and in urban constituencies in the south of England. Ironically Disraeli presided over two nations at the time of his greatest triumph.

The formation of Disraeli's great ministry immediately following Gladstone's made the 1870s a decisive decade in party political development. Before that the configuration of parties had been complicated by cross currents. Afterwards Britain was so divided into two parties that Gilbert and Sullivan were not unduly exaggerating when they claimed that every child was born 'either a little Liberal or else a little Conservative'.

The Conservatives used their first spell of real power since the 1840s to deal with issues with which they had not been previously associated. Indeed the year 1874 saw a spate of statutes dealing with social problems. An Agricultural Holdings Act took a leaf out of Gladstone's Irish Land Act by giving tenants in Britain the right to be compensated for improvements made during their tenancies. An Artisan's Dwelling Act gave some eighty-seven town councils the authority to demolish slums and replace them with better housing. Trades unions benefited from the Employers and Workmen Act and the Protection of Property Act. The first changed the legal basis of industrial relations from the inequitable concept of master and servant to one which recognised the worker's freedom of contract and right to collective bargaining, while the second legalised peaceful picketing. Other acts consolidated public health legislation, safeguarded the funds of friendly societies, and protected women and children in factories.

The legislation has been attributed to Disraelian concern with 'Tory democracy'. But the prime minister did not even have a programme, let alone a philosophy. At best he was a pragmatist, at worst an opportunist. The main inspiration behind the statutes was not his but the home secretary, R. A. Cross. Cross, who had been educated at Rugby and Cambridge and became a banker and a magistrate, was scarcely the man to advocate measures detrimental to the established order. Insofar as the trade union legislation was more than a remedy for an anachronistic legal framework, it was calculated to appeal to a movement which felt itself to have been let down by the previous government. The Criminal Law Amendment Act of 1871 had made picketing virtually illegal. Trade unionists, who had previously been inclined to support the Liberals, deserted them at the polls in 1874 and might even have voted for Tory candidates, especially if they offered to support the repeal of the obnoxious law. In this respect the two trade union acts redeemed election pledges. Not that the bid for the labour vote was successful in the long run. Despite the fact that in 1880 even a Liberal admitted that the Conservatives had done more for the working man in five years than his party had done in fifty, the unions reverted to their former allegiance in the general election held that year. Why working men deserted the Tories in 1880 is unclear. The run-up to the election is so often rehearsed in terms of a debate between the two parties over foreign policy that it tends to be assumed that the voters were swayed by this dispute. Yet the assumption cannot be tested conclusively. It could be that the deepening economic depression hurt the Conservatives more, especially among the working class, than any concern over the alleged immorality of their relations with other powers. Curiously the Conservatives themselves placed little emphasis on any credit they could claim from their social reforms, and mainly defended their foreign policy. They seem to have been convinced that their adoption of Palmerstonian postures, now identified as 'jingoism' from a popular song of the day, would have more electoral appeal than Liberal denunciations of it.

The principal arena in which their activities had been criticised was the Balkans. Ever since the Crimean War British policy had been committed to shoring up the crumbling Ottoman Empire in order to prevent Russia from picking up the crumbs. In 1876 this policy backfired when the Turks suppressed an uprising of Orthodox Christians in Bulgaria with extreme ferocity, massacring thousands. Disraeli tried to play down the incident, but the 'Bulgarian horrors' provoked a public outcry. The outrage was fanned by petitions and public meetings, largely organised by nonconformists, and by reports in the press of which those of W. T. Stead in the Darlington-based *Northern Echo* were especially effective. Public indignation roused Gladstone, who saw an opportunity to unite the Liberals against Disraeli. Liberal disarray in the 1874 election had so dispirited him that early in the new parliament he had stood down from the leadership of the party, resigning it to the Whigs, Granville in the Lords and Hartington in the Commons. Gladstone had even announced his desire for an interval of retirement between parliament and the grave. But moral indignation and political calculation made another gladiatorial combat with the Conservative leader, whom by now he cordially hated, irresistible. The 'Grand Old Man' entered the lists with a pamphlet entitled *Bulgarian Horrors and the Question of the East*. It sold 40,000 copies within days of its publication. 'From that time forward,' he wrote years later, 'till the final consummation in 1879–80, I made the eastern question the main business of my life.' The Bulgarian agitation alienated the Whig leaders of the Liberal party, who resented what they saw as Gladstone's deliberate sabotaging of their leadership with a demagogic bid to wrest it from them. They were not sorry when an attempt on his part to force the government to impose reforms on Turkey was defeated. Their suspicions that Gladstone was moving closer to the radical wing of the party seemed to be confirmed when he accepted an invitation to attend the formative meeting of the National Liberal Federation in 1877. He shared the platform at Birmingham with the driving force behind the Federation, the radical MP Joseph Chamberlain.

Disraeli himself defused the eastern question as an immediate issue at the Congress of Berlin in 1878. The prime minister, who had been made Earl of Beaconsfield, went in person and could claim some credit for the successful outcome. Had he got Queen Victoria to dissolve parliament at this juncture he might have led the Conservatives to another victory. His personal reputation was at its height, not only on account of his triumph at Berlin but also through his purchase for

Britain of the Khedive of Egypt's shares in the Suez Canal, and his attainment of the title Empress of India for the queen. A 'snap' election to cash in on his popularity was, however, ruled out.

The decision to postpone a dissolution was to prove fatal. For meanwhile fresh disasters arose, external and internal. Abroad imperial commitments in India and South Africa generated friction on their frontiers. Hostilities broke out in Afghanistan and Zululand which culminated in the loss of British lives. Although Disraeli could not reasonably be held responsible for these events, Gladstone made political capital out of them, denouncing 'Beaconsfieldism' as he rather cumbrously called it. More damaging, perhaps, was the depression in the domestic economy, causing unemployment to rise and the price of wheat to slump in 1879. Industrialists and farmers clamoured for protection, but Disraeli declined to respond.

Gladstone castigated the government's record in his 'whistle stop' trip to Edinburgh late in 1879, the so-called 'Midlothian campaign'. He dwelt on the disasters abroad, for the Liberals had no more of a remedy for the recession than had the Tories.

Disraeli could have delayed the dissolution until February 1881. Instead he decided on a snap election early in 1880 when two by-elections, at Liverpool and Southwark, seemed to indicate a swing to the Conservatives. Yet when a general election was held there was a 5 per cent swing back to the Liberals over the 1874 results. There was a higher turn-out, with over 3 million votes being cast for the first time. The Liberals obtained 56 per cent of them, gaining 351 seats to the Conservatives' 239. They reduced the Tories to the low level of 1868 in Scotland and almost drove them out of Wales. Several county seats fell to them, and had they fielded more candidates several more shires might have gone to the Liberals. The rout was not as complete in the larger towns as it had been in 1868. Nevertheless the outcome of the contest was a trouncing for Beaconsfieldism. Disraeli himself did not live to fight another day, dying in 1881.

As he went down to defeat he raised warnings about the problem of home rule for Ireland. Gladstone dismissed them, holding the Conservatives responsible for the alienation of the Irish. Nevertheless where fifty-seven Home Rulers had been returned in 1874, sixty-two were elected in 1880. They found a charismatic leader in Charles Stewart Parnell, who led the majority of the Irish MPs at Westminster for the next decade. He was also president of the Land League formed in 1879 to take up the cause of tenants in Ireland. The agricultural depression hit Irish farming with particular severity after the failure of the harvest in 1879. The lowering of prices brought about by the import of cheaper foreign foodstuffs meant that many tenants could not afford to pay their rents. Rent strikes ensued, provoking reprisals from landlords. The Land League retaliated, and 'outrages', the favoured Victorian word for acts of violence involving Irishmen, flared up.

Gladstone's government reacted to these problems with a carrot and a stick. The carrot was another Land Act which recognised tenants' claims known as the 'three Fs': fair rents; fixity of tenure; and free sale of the rights of occupancy. The stick was a Coercion Act which gave the viceroy draconian powers. Parnell exploited every obstructive tactic he could to hold up the bill's progress, prolonging one sitting of the Commons to forty-one hours in January 1881. The procedures of the House had to be changed to allow the closure of debates in order to prevent such obstruction in future. In October Parnell was imprisoned under the terms of the Coercion Act for his association with the Land League's campaign of violence. The consequence was to provoke further 'outrages', culminating in the murders of the viceroy and his secretary in Phoenix Park, Dublin in May 1882. Parnell, however, who had been released from prison a few days earlier, totally disowned the perpetrators and acted as a mediator between the British and the aggrieved Irish. His efforts helped to turn the tide of violence in the summer of 1882, though an improvement in the underlying conditions which had given rise to it also made the next few years more tranquil.

Gladstone realised that the Land Act of 1881 had not 'reached the core' of the Irish question, but thought he had 'made a long step towards the solution' by including Ireland in the Franchise Act of 1884. This was the first reform act which applied to the whole United Kingdom. It enfranchised all voters in English and Welsh counties and in Ireland and Scotland, on the basis of the borough franchise established in England by the second Reform Act. Thus ratepaying householders, lodgers paying £10 or more a year in rent, and occupiers of lands or tenements worth £10 a year, were entitled to vote provided they had been resident for twelve months. The result was a dramatic increase in the electorate. In England and Wales it expanded from

2,600,000 to 4,400,000, or roughly two-thirds of adult males. In Scotland the effect was to enfranchise about 60 per cent of the adult male population. But the increase was especially noticeable in Ireland, where 50 per cent of all men were allowed the vote compared with one in six after the second Reform Act.

The overall increase of the electorate alarmed the Conservatives. They feared that an election held on this basis in the existing constituencies would reduce them to permanent opposition, which had nearly been their fate after 1832. Unable to prevent the bill's passage through the Commons they mustered enough strength in the House of Lords to defeat it in July 1884. The motion was that such a measure should be accompanied by 'provisions for so apportioning the right to return members as to insure a true and fair representation of the people'. In other words they wanted a redistribution of seats which would redress the balance in their favour.

The rejection of the Franchise Bill by the peers led to an attack on their privileges by its more radical supporters. Even Gladstone, who called a special autumn session of parliament to reintroduce it, called for demonstrations over the summer. An estimated 100,000 workers marched through London on 21 July. This and most other demonstrations passed off peacefully, but there was a riot at Aston Park in Birmingham when Liberals gatecrashed a Tory rally. The demonstrations, however, if anything stiffened the resolve of the Conservatives to throw the bill out again unless it were accompanied by one for redistribution of seats.

A novel way out of the impasse was found when the party leaders agreed to meet at Downing Street to thrash out a scheme for redrawing constituency boundaries. After the constitutional crisis this solution produced something of a farce, with maps strewn all over the floor of the room while Gladstone and the Marquis of Salisbury, Disraeli's successor as Tory leader, with four of their colleagues, pored over them. Salisbury proved most adroit at horse trading, coming away with a good deal for his party. The outcome was an agreement that boroughs with under 15,000 inhabitants would lose their separate representation, while those with between 15,000 and 50,000 would lose one seat. This produced a total of 138 seats to be redistributed. Ninety-four of these were allocated to counties, while the rest were given to populous cities. Thus London increased its number of representatives from twenty-two to sixty-two. The boundary commissioners who implemented the intentions of the act were instructed as far as possible to create homogeneous constituencies, distinguishing not only between rural and urban districts but also, in effect, between middle-class suburbia and working-class streets. The result was to give the Conservatives an in-built advantage, offsetting the Liberal bias which had operated in the constituencies created by previous reform acts.

Sweeping though the changes were, it cannot be said that the Franchise and Redistribution Acts brought democracy to Britain. As we have seen, the proportion of adult males eligible to vote even in theory was between a half and two-thirds. In practice it was a good deal lower than this, because of the technicalities of registration. Hardly any lodgers, for instance, got on to the electoral register despite the intentions of the second and third Reform Acts to include them. At most only 50 per cent of adult males actually registered even in England and Wales. A proposal to enfranchise women got nowhere. Britain had still a long way to go before achieving full democracy.

The Redistribution Act brought into being the norm of single-member constituencies. Both the radical and Whig wings of the Liberal party disliked this, since multi-member constituencies had enabled them to share their representation. After 1867, for instance, Birmingham along with other cities had three seats. Careful organisation by the 'caucus' directed by Joseph Chamberlain had ensured that all three were captured by Liberal candidates. However, Gladstone was convinced that contests between rival Liberal candidates had played into Conservative hands, and welcomed this change since it ensured straight two-party fights. The act also upheld the 'first past the post' system, whereby the candidate with the highest number rather than the majority of votes cast is returned. Advocates of proportional representation criticised this at the time, but their advocacy received even shorter shrift from the Commons than the proposal to give votes to women.

The first general election under the new arrangements was held in November 1885. At the time of the dissolution a Conservative ministry led by Lord Salisbury was in office, the Tories having defeated Gladstone's budget in June. Salisbury's ministry was, however, seen as a caretaker government until the new electoral registers were ready and a contest could take place. The polls witnessed a turn-out of 81 per cent, the highest of the nineteenth century, and the lowest number of uncontested seats. Not much was made in Britain of the Irish question which was to dominate the new parliament. Instead religion was the most pressing issue, especially in Scotland. In addition Joseph Chamberlain and other radicals put forward proposals for free education, cheap housing and land reform. The results gave the Liberals 335 seats and the Conservatives 249. Once again Liberals were more successful in Scotland and Wales, where they took 89 per cent of the seats, than in England, where they obtained 53 per cent. They made rather more headway in English counties than usual, perhaps because they had enfranchised agricultural labourers who now voted for the first time. On the other hand the Conservatives made inroads into the urban, and especially the suburban, constituencies.

The results from Ireland, however, transformed the situation. There Parnell's nationalists took virtually all before them, winning eighty-five seats. Only the Conservatives prevented a clean sweep, by taking seventeen Ulster seats, for the Liberals were annihilated in Ireland.

Parnell's eighty-six supporters – including one from Liverpool – exactly held the balance between the British parties at Westminster. The question was which way they would swing it. Parnell himself had actually urged Irish voters in Britain to support Conservative candidates. Since few were registered, however, this was probably counterproductive. When Salisbury indicated that he would favour coercion in Ireland, while Gladstone hinted in what became known as 'the Hawarden kite' that he would support home rule, the balance inevitably tipped towards the Liberals. Salisbury was ousted and Gladstone formed his third administration early in 1886.

The Home Rule Bill which Gladstone introduced was a modest measure. 'Imperial' affairs, which were to include foreign policy and indirect taxation, were to be retained at Westminster. The Irish were to be autonomous within this framework, having responsibility for affairs affecting their country only. And yet they were not to continue to be represented in the parliament of the United Kingdom. This provoked a rebellion from Gladstone's own supporters, who called themselves 'Liberal Unionists' because they were not prepared to dissolve the Union. Ninety-four of them voted with the Conservatives to defeat the bill at its second reading. Gladstone's government fell as a result.

The Liberal Unionists rebellion cut right across the ideological

17   'His First Vote', a patronising view of the newly enfranchised agricultural labourer

fissures in the party. Joseph Chamberlain, the radical leader, was one of the principal rebels along with Lord Hartington, the most prominent Whig. At one level they were the losers in a game fought with Gladstone for the high stakes of the leadership of the Liberal party. Rather more Whigs than radicals rebelled, which has been seen as the occasion of the final departure of the Whig landlords from the Liberal party to their natural habitat on the Conservative benches, ensuring that Liberalism became more radical. Yet a close analysis of the split shows that all sections of the party, moderate Liberals as well as Whigs and radicals, both joined the rebels and remained loyal to Gladstone. He was thus left with a cross-section of the party which had triumphed at the polls in 1885 rather than with a radical rump.

His much reduced forces, however, were far from being triumphant in the general election which Gladstone called immediately after the defeat of his Home Rule Bill. Conservatives co-operated with Liberal Unionists, not opposing them in constituencies where they could defeat a Gladstonian Liberal unless a Conservative candidate intervened. Conservatives and Liberal Unionists trounced Gladstonian Liberals in the south of England, driving them back into their strongholds in the north, Scotland and Wales. Scottish and Welsh voters, however, demonstrated their loyalty to Gladstone not only by opposing Conservative candidates but also by supporting Liberals against Liberal Unionists.

The result was that the Conservatives emerged as the largest single party in the Commons, with 317 seats. The Gladstonian Liberals formed the second party with 191. The Irish Nationalists held their own with 85. Liberal Unionists numbered 77, making them the smallest party in the House. Yet they were numerous enough either to keep the Conservatives in office even if they merely abstained, or to outnumber them if they joined with their former colleagues and the Parnellites. The Liberal party had frequently split before, allowing the Conservatives brief spells in office until it united again. This time, however, the division was permanent, giving the Conservatives a run of twenty years in power with the brief exception of the Liberal government of 1892 to 1895. The third Marquis of Salisbury, who succeeded Gladstone as prime minister, welcomed the secession of the Liberal Unionists from his rival's ranks, a development which he had long anticipated. For Salisbury was perhaps unique in politicians of the first rank in the nineteenth century to accept that the main dynamic of politics was class antagonism. He foresaw a coming clash between the propertied classes and the masses, and knew instinctively which side he and the Conservative party should take. It irked him that many Whig landowners, for reasons of family history rather than self-interest, stayed in the Liberal party despite it also housing radicals of the stamp of John Bright, who preached class war against aristocrats, and Joseph Chamberlain, who once described Salisbury himself as being of the class which, like the lilies of the field, neither toiled nor spun. Although ironically Chamberlain and Bright had seceded from the Liberals along with the Liberal Unionists, their colleagues included the bulk of those whose alliance with the Conservatives the new prime minister had encouraged.

Although they were prepared to keep his government in power they were not ready to join in a coalition until 1895. Salisbury had therefore to construct his first ministry from his own supporters. He himself took not the customary first lordship of the treasury but, unusually, the foreign secretaryship. Since he was a peer his choice of leader of the Commons was crucial. After Disraeli's promotion to the peerage the Conservatives in the Commons had been led by Sir Stafford Northcote, but his incompetence had frayed the patience of some younger MPs who had formed what became known, at first in jest, as the Fourth party. They had managed to ensure that Salisbury rather than Northcote led the party to its electoral victory in 1886. When he became prime minister, therefore, Salisbury had a debt of gratitude to this group. Outstanding among them was Lord Randolph Churchill, whom Salisbury made not only leader of the House but also chancellor of the exchequer.

Churchill represented a new breed of Conservative who welcomed rather than shrank from the prospect of democracy. He greatly admired Bismarck, who presided over a conservative regime in the newly united Germany despite, or perhaps because of, its democratic electoral system. Churchill's controversial chairmanship of the National Union of Conservative Associations gave him an opportunity to put his concept of 'Tory democracy' into practice. His impatient ambition made him a thorn in Salisbury's flesh, or, as the prime minister put it, a boil in the back of his neck. In December 1886 Churchill resigned from the chancellorship in protest at the naval estimates. This was a calculated bid for the leadership. He even toyed with the idea of a coalition of Chamberlain radicals and Churchillian Conservatives in a new party. But his bid failed because he over-estimated the strength of his own position and underestimated that of Salisbury. It was the prime minister who made the first move towards a realignment of parties by getting the Liberal Unionist Goschen to replace Churchill as chancellor. After his fall Churchill rapidly declined as the ravages of syphilis and his resort to alcohol and medication to offset them took their toll.

There was to be no other serious challenge to Salisbury's leadership. When he left office in 1902 it was as a result of retirement rather than a defeat in parliament or at the polls. His was the first such resignation of the premiership for over a century.

Salisbury's feat was the more remarkable as he felt himself to be out of touch with the times. So far from representing a new breed of Conservative he embodied old-fashioned toryism. He was devoted to the queen and the monarchy and to the Church of England. Indeed it has been claimed that his 'religious policy as prime minister was his highest priority'. Thus he was prepared to subsidise the denomi-national elementary schools by making access to them free in 1891, since to him they served a more moral purpose than the board schools. Religion was necessary to provide a social cement to offset the disintegrating effect of the drift towards democracy. Although he dreaded the drift, he regarded it as inevitable. All that Conservatives could hope to do was to control it. Where Churchill admired Bismarck's success in achieving that in Germany, Salisbury came to appreciate the constitution of the United States of America with its checks and balances on the tyranny of the majority. Britain did not have the safeguard of a Supreme Court, which in his opinion would have declared some of Gladstone's Irish legislation unconstitutional. But it did have a House of Lords and a Conservative party which could serve a similar function.

The House of Lords was employed to reject legislation passed by the Commons in Gladstone's last ministry. Salisbury could claim that the Liberals did not have a mandate for their measures since the outcome of the 1892 elections was so indecisive that he even stayed in office until defeated on a vote of no confidence in the new parliament. The results gave the Liberals the most seats, 272, but only just, as the Conservatives obtained 268. They were therefore dependent upon the Irish nationalists, who gained 80 seats. They would scarcely support Salisbury following the coercive policy adopted towards Ireland by his nephew Arthur Balfour. But they were demoralised after their leader Parnell had been discredited by his citation as co-respondent in a divorce case in 1890. Although the Liberal Unionists were reduced to only 46 seats Salisbury could claim that there was a majority in Britain, and especially in England, where the Conservatives and their allies held 57 per cent of the seats, for the preservation of the Union. Consequently when Gladstone's Home Rule Bill passed the Commons he had no qualms about leading opposition to it in the Lords which threw it out by 419 votes to 41. Gladstone could have called Salisbury's bluff by asking the queen for a dissolution, in order to fight an election on a platform of people versus peers; but there was no bluff to call. Instead he clung on to office for another six months, then resigned, leaving Lord Rosebery to face inevitable defeat on a vote in the Commons in 1895.

The queen asked Salisbury to form a government. His second ministry was a coalition of Conservatives and Liberal Unionists from the start. He again took the foreign secretaryship himself, giving the first lordship of the treasury to Balfour. He then offered four seats in the cabinet to the Liberal Unionists, to fill as they liked. To his surprise Joseph Chamberlain chose the colonial secretaryship. As soon as the ministry was formed Salisbury got the queen to dissolve parliament.

A victory for the Conservatives and Liberal Unionists was a foregone conclusion, since the demoralised Liberals did not even contest 130 seats. But the scale of the triumph surprised Salisbury himself, since it gave the Conservatives an overall majority, causing him to regret his generous treatment of the Liberal Unionists in the distribution of posts in the coalition government. The landslide of seats, however, did not reflect a seismic shift of votes. The electoral system established in 1884 and 1885 could produce great changes in the composition of the Commons with only slight swings in voting behaviour. It has been estimated that the outcome of the 1895 election represented a swing of only 3 per cent to the Conservatives and Liberal Unionists. With such a small margin such considerations as organisation, money and press support were crucial. The Conservative machine had been overhauled by R. E. Middleton, whose efforts in the constituencies were rewarded by the party with a cheque for £10,000 at a banquet held after the triumph. In addition to the professionally organised National Union of Conservative Associations there was the hugely successful voluntary organisation of the Primrose League, founded in 1884, which had over a million members by 1895. These efforts replaced the activities of the magnates who had controlled elections at their own vast expense, until the Corrupt Practices Act of 1883 severely limited the amounts of money which candidates could spend. Before that Liberal candidates had on the whole been better financed, given the wealth of the Whig grandees. Their secession from the party, however, ensured that their rivals commanded more cash thereafter. Again the press had tended to lean towards the Liberals in Gladstone's heyday, whereas during the 1890s it veered more towards the Conservatives. All these considerations helped Salisbury to obtain the first overall Conservative majority since 1874.

The Independent Labour party, founded two years earlier, put up only twenty-eight candidates, all of whom were defeated. Yet Salisbury saw socialism as a distinct threat to the capitalist system, and gave priority to social reforms as a means of avoiding it. Soon after the general election he announced publicly that 'we have got, as far as we can, to make this country more pleasant to live in for the vast majority'. He dealt with labour problems with the Conciliation Act of 1896 which allowed the board of trade to arbitrate between employers and employees, and with a scheme to compensate workers injured in industrial accidents. His government also passed measures aimed at improving public health and working conditions. He even promoted a scheme to introduce old age pensions, but the actuarial work on it foundered with the soaring costs incurred by the outbreak of the Boer War.

Such proposals anticipated the class-based politics of the twentieth century. In the 1890s they raised little controversy in comparison with religious issues which were still more divisive. They certainly threatened to divide Salisbury's coalition when an education bill put forward in 1896 upset the Liberal Unionists because it alienated nonconformists. It was proposed to set up educational committees in counties and county boroughs to supervise all schools, both those administered by the local authority boards and those run by religious denominations. Although more financial aid was offered to denominational schools, the prospect of bureaucratic control proved unacceptable to the government's own supporters and the bill had to be dropped.

The Unionist coalition survived the crisis partly because it remained united on the question of Ireland. Their policy, born of cynicism more than altruism, was 'to kill home rule with kindness'. Successive Land Purchase Acts to enable tenants to buy their holdings sought to buy off the kind of agitation which was exploited by the United Land League, founded by William O'Brien in 1898. That year also saw the passing of the Irish Local Government Act which introduced the new British system of county councils and rural and urban district councils. Although the Nationalists took three-quarters of the seats in the first elections they did not regard it as a substitute for home rule. On the contrary Irish nationalism was roused against British imperialism, especially after the outbreak of the Boer War, producing a closing of the ranks of the parliamentary party under the leadership of John Redmond, a former Parnellite.

Imperialism strained rather than cemented the alliance of the Conservative prime minister and his Liberal Unionist colonial secretary, Joseph Chamberlain. In his capacity as foreign secretary Salisbury sought to protect Britain's recently acquired imperial interests rather than her traditional international concerns. Thus in the Mediterranean Britain had become accustomed to side with France to defend Turkey against Russian expansion. But by the late nineteenth century French naval power was seen as a threat to Britain's presence in Egypt. Salisbury was therefore anxious to disengage from defending Turkey and to concentrate on supporting Egyptian commitments. In 1898 Franco-British imperial rivalry nearly led to hostilities in the Sudan when military expeditions from the two countries clashed at Fashoda.

Yet Salisbury was not a militant imperialist. When news reached him that the British expedition had defeated a Sudanese force two weeks before the Fashoda incident he wrote: 'A slaughter of 16,000 ought to satisfy our Jingoes for at least six months.' Among the jingoists was Chamberlain, who demonstrated his zeal for imperial expansion in southern Africa. He was implicated in the Jameson raid in 1895, when an attack on the Boer republic of the Transvaal was repulsed. To add insult to injury, the German emperor sent a telegram to congratulate Kruger the president of the Transvaal on the defeat of the raid. Friction between British colonists at the Cape and the Boers in the interior was largely due to the discovery of gold and diamonds in the vicinity of Johannesburg. Thousands of colonists flocked there hoping to get rich quick. The British high commissioner at Cape Town, Sir Alfred Milner, used their presence to put pressure on Kruger to grant them civil rights. Seeing this as a Trojan horse Kruger made a pre-emptive strike against the British in 1899. The Boer War had begun.

At first it went badly for Britain. So far from requiring only a small expeditionary force to crush the Boers within a few weeks, the conflict grew into a major confrontation lasting over two years. Some 22,000 troops out of 447,000 on the British side died of wounds or disease. The financial cost came to £200,000,000. The loss of prestige was even greater. Not only had the greatest power on earth been humiliated by a small republic of farmers, but the methods used to ensure ultimate victory tarnished her claim to moral superiority. To defeat guerillas the British adopted a scorched-earth policy, clearing whole regions of inhabitants and confining them in 'concentration camps' in which between 18,000 and 28,000 people died.

The occupation of the Transvaal by August 1900 persuaded the prime minister to call a general election. Yet Salisbury himself did not attempt to cash in on the apparent final victory over the Boers. His own election address was low-key, arguing that divisions in the Liberal party made it unfit for government. It was left to Chamberlain to whip up jingoist hysteria with the claim that 'every seat lost to the government is a seat gained to the Boers'. The resulting contest at the polls has ever since been known as the 'khaki' election. How far it marked the triumph of jingoism, however, can be disputed. The overall Unionist majority fell by eighteen seats over the total they won in 1895. The number of uncontested seats rose while the turn-out where there were contests fell, so that the total number of votes cast went down by more than a million. On the other hand the Unionists obtained a higher percentage of the votes cast, achieving the rare feat of polling over half of them. Moreover they obtained a majority of the Scottish seats, a unique achievement for Conservatives and their allies, and all but eight of the London seats, while many working-class constituencies, such as Brightside, Sheffield, deserted the Liberal camp. This was achieved against a recent by-election trend of victories to their opponents, unlike the situation five years earlier. The election thus halted the swing of the

18   'The khaki campaign: a surrender', the radical carpenter
seduced by the patriotic siren

19   Queen Victoria in old age

pendulum which had brought parliamentary majorities to each party at alternative elections since 1868, giving the Conservatives and Liberal Unionists two victories over the Liberals and others in succession.

Salisbury, now aged seventy-one, wanted to step down as prime minister, but as he explained when he eventually resigned in 1902, 'I have contemplated taking this step on grounds of health for some time; but have been deterred from it by the fear that, so long as the war continued, I might give an impression that there was a division in the cabinet.' That this was not a mere excuse can be concluded from his giving up the foreign secretaryship when he formed his last administration after the general election. Whatever lingering ambition might have remained was extinguished when Victoria died in 1901. There had been a firm bond between the prime minister and the queen. By contrast he had little regard for Edward VII. Salisbury was essentially a Victorian. His resignation marked the end of an era in politics as much as the death of the queen did in the life of the nation.

6

Twentieth-century Britain

Just as some historians have argued for a 'long eighteenth century', extending to 1832, so claims have been made for a 'long nineteenth century', ending after the chronological terminus of 1900. Certainly the case for commencing the history of Britain in the twentieth century with the general election of 1906 has its attractions, while a stronger claim still can be made for stretching the Victorian period to include the Edwardian and even the pre-war years which came to an abrupt end in 1914. Undoubtedly the First World War was, and was seen as, a watershed in British history. Nevertheless the earlier war with which the twentieth century opened, the conflict with the Boers in southern Africa, also marked enough of a turning point to justify starting an account of post-Victorian Britain around the time of the death of Queen Victoria herself.

For the Boer War jolted Victorian confidence in progress. The brash assumptions, verging on arrogance, that history, if not providence, had singled out the British to be its favoured children, to provide the rest of the world with the model of material and moral improvement, had received some hard knocks since its heyday in 1851, the year of the Great Exhibition. The challenge of economic competitors, particularly Germany and the United States, had raised doubts about their material superiority, while the perceived decadence of the nineties undermined claims to moral leadership. Yet belief in British superiority had stubbornly survived. A conflict in which the greatest imperial power in the world could be resisted for three years by a handful of settlers, however, seemed to confirm the sad decline of the country from its commanding position in the middle of the nineteenth century.

One manifestation of this appeared to be the appalling physical condition of the recruits who offered themselves for service in the war. Many had to be rejected as being unfit after medical tests which were none too stringent. Some alarmists even concluded that this was proof of the British race being degenerate. Such fears gave rise to the establishment of an interdepartmental committee on physical degeneration in 1903. Racists attributed the alleged degeneracy to hereditary racial characteristics. Most commentators, however, blamed the effects of an industrial environment on the health of the working class. They acknowledged that, while middle-class families were clearly limiting their size, working-class parents were not practising any form of family limitation and were therefore having more children. They also pointed out that infant mortality in the country at large was around 105 per 1,000, whereas in the great conurbations it was about 200.

By 1901 some 78 per cent of the population of 37 million lived in cities and towns. Social conditions in urban areas had undoubtedly improved since the dreadful squalor and insanitary state they stood in at the accession of Victoria. This was not only the case in the new middle-class 'suburbs' but also in poorer parts of towns. Clean water and effective drainage eliminated cholera and other health risks associated with the basic lack of hygiene. Standards of living had also risen, and with them life expectancy. Nevertheless nutritional standards, especially among the unskilled labourers and their families, were largely responsible for the poor physical condition of the volunteers for active service in the Boer War. Bad housing also contributed to the high incidence of bronchitis, tuberculosis and other chest complaints which afflicted them.

These conditions were not drastically changed in the years between that conflict and the outbreak of the First World War. When a new round of recruitment started people were once again appalled at the numbers who had to be rejected for being undersized, underweight and generally unfit for active or indeed for any military service. Ironically those so rejected stood a better chance of living longer than they would have done had there been no war, for nutritional standards rose during the war years not only in general but particularly for the semi-skilled and unskilled workers. The 'dilution' of labour during the war years, whereby trade unions allowed semi-skilled workers to do skilled work, meant that many could command better wages than they had done previously, and since prices did not rise commensurately, they could afford more nutritious foods.

Those who were accepted by the army, on the other hand, had the worst life expectancies of the century. This affected above all the upper classes, since few were deemed to be unfit and most served as junior officers, who were the most vulnerable groups in the fighting. Casualties among commissioned officers were so high as to give some credence to the notion of a 'lost generation' brought about by the First World War. The total carnage of nearly three-quarters of a million dead left a psychological scar which lasted longer than a generation.

The intense patriotism which this sacrifice provoked was also anticipated during the Boer War. Thus the 'khaki' election of 1900 was characterised by the same kind of enthusiasm and blind jingoism which accompanied the call to the colours in 1914. War memorials with their lists of men who had 'fallen' during the conflict were erected in 1902 as well as in 1919. Such sentiments were far more powerful than the voices raised against imperialism and nationalism during the wars, or the slogans of class struggle shouted between them. They expressed profound loyalties to king and country even, or perhaps especially, among the poorer classes of society.

And yet Britain continued to be a class-conscious country. The war memorials listed the 'fallen' officers first, the NCOs and privates last, as though class distinctions were drawn by death itself. For the officers came from the upper classes, particularly those families who sent their sons to the public schools and the ancient universities. Traditionally these were landed families who formed the backbone of a ruling class. But the impact of the 'great depression' of the 1890s on landed incomes had caused land to lose its attractiveness as an investment. Of course it had always had more than an economic appeal, granting social status and political influence to its owners. But even these perquisites of landownership seemed to lose some of their kudos. People became more ready to sell as well as to buy land, and something like a quarter of the estates of Britain changed hands in the years immediately after the Great War. Thereafter the ruling class was less obviously landed. Thus the Conservative party in parliament at the end of the 1920s drew only 14 per cent of its MPs from landed backgrounds, compared with 32 per cent from business and 35 per cent from the professions. At the same time roughly half of them had been to major public schools, while 45 per cent were graduates of Oxford or Cambridge.

Education, indeed, became more of a clue to class distinctions than sources of wealth. Six per cent of the nation's schoolchildren were privately educated. In 1918 the rest were required to receive compulsory education to the age of fourteen. This was provided for most in free 'elementary' schools, while a small minority also went to 'secondary' schools, where fees were paid. Various proposals were made between the wars to raise the school-leaving age to fifteen and to provide free education for all, but these were not fully implemented until the Education Act of 1944. This act took as its basic assumption that there were innate abilities in children. Some, a minority, were 'academic'. These should be encouraged to go to grammar schools. Others had technical skills, and should go to appropriate schools for training. The rest should receive a basic education in secondary modern schools. Examinations were held at the age of eleven to decide which kind of secondary education was more suitable after primary school. These psychological assumptions had class implications. Middle-class children, who were regarded as innately 'academic', mainly went to grammar schools. Technical schools were intended for the children of the skilled working class, though very few local authorities made provision for such schooling. Most working-class children, whether from skilled, semi-skilled or unskilled backgrounds, went to the secondary modern schools.

The educational system tended to reinforce sexual as well as social stereotypes. One of the criticisms of the selection of secondary education by the examination of eleven-year-old children was that proportionately more places were made available for boys than for girls in grammar schools, even though statistically girls performed better than boys in tests at that age. The assumption was that boys would proceed to higher education and enter business or the professions, while girls would leave schools for temporary jobs before marrying and becoming full-time wives and mothers. This was at odds with the growth of opportunities for women in the twentieth century. In 1911 some 590,000 were employed in business and the professions. The First World War doubled this number.

The wartime gains of women, however, were shortlived. Between 1914 and 1918 some 1,345,000 women entered the labour force to replace men recruited for service abroad. They found employment in jobs which had previously had few or no female workers. In the late nineteenth century middle-class women who sought careers had to find them as governesses or teachers, while girls from the lower classes overwhelmingly went into domestic service. Now they found jobs on farms, in factories, in hospitals, in offices and in transport. The unions, suspicious of women as a pool of cheap labour, and anxious to ensure that servicemen regained their jobs when they returned home, treated them coolly. By and large they did leave work when the war ended. Where they had been urged by the press to obtain employment, especially in munitions factories, they were harassed to leave when they were no longer needed. Many returned to domestic service, for although the numbers of servants per household dropped dramatically in the 1920s as 'labour-saving' devices replaced them, nevertheless the number of households with servants increased between the wars. The war, therefore, did little to boost the upward trend in the numbers of the female population in employment, which rose anyway from just over 4 million in 1901 to 5,600,000 by 1931.

Contrary to a widely held view, the war did not do much to gain recognition of women's contribution by obtaining the vote for them. It did not persuade politicians that since women could do men's work then they were fit to take on other male roles too. The young munitions girls would have to wait some years before achieving the age of thirty at which, after 1918, women could vote in parliamentary elections. They might have to wait even longer to become ratepayers or the wives of ratepayers, which was a further qualification required by the act. It was not until 1928 that women were enfranchised on the same basis as men.

When women did vote, however, they tended to boost the conservative element among the electorate. Female enfranchisement reinforced the forces of inertia in British society which have preserved its institutions and class structure despite the strains of social and economic change. That they survived the inter-war period of high unemployment and trade union militancy is something of a paradox. Yet in fact the twenties and especially the thirties were decades of increasing prosperity for the majority of the working class who

20   King George V making his first Christmas broadcast in 1932

managed to stay in employment. This section of the community benefited from the production of consumer goods in the new electrical and engineering industries. The manufacture of gramophones and records, radios (or wirelesses as they were called), electric irons and vacuum cleaners created something of a consumer boom, since by the late 1930s most households had acquired them. The production of motor cars also created employment, though their purchase was largely confined to the middle class, motor and pedal cycles being the working man's private means of transport. The rise in the standard of living of the workers widened the gap between 'respectable' and 'rough' families. Households where the husband and even the wife frequented public houses, while their children were dressed in rags and either clogs or no shoes at all, became far less prevalent than they had been before the First World War. The gains of semi-skilled and unskilled workers during the war were set back by the mass unemployment between the world wars, though their standard of living was not reduced to its pre-war level. This was partly due to the provision by the national government of unemployment benefits and by local authorities of council housing which replaced slums. The life-styles of skilled workers who managed to stay in work improved dramatically. Many if not most afforded new clothes for their offspring at Whitsuntide, visiting their neighbours to show them off and to be given a penny. Many also went on annual holidays to the seaside. The ability of working-class families to afford these 'luxuries' was partly the result of their limiting the numbers of their children. Birth control, which before 1914 had been practised largely by the upper and middle classes, now became widespread throughout society.

The new industries brought prosperity to the districts in which they were located, most of them being in the midlands and the south-east of England. Increasingly the nation was being divided into two economic areas, one of prosperity, the other of depression. Where older declining industries predominated, in the textile districts of the north, the shipbuilding ports of the north-east and Scotland, and the coalfields of south Wales, Yorkshire and County Durham, unemployment levels soared way above the national average. These were the regions of despair and hunger marches. Many left them to seek work in the more prosperous south. As a result the population trends of the past two centuries were reversed, with migration readjusting the balance from the older industrial areas of the north, Scotland and Wales towards the midlands and the home counties. This led to fears that the heartlands of the industrial revolution would become wastelands in which despair could lead to political discontent.

Despair indeed led to depression and desperation. Unemployed men were driven to suicide, perhaps as many as two a week on average in the early 1930s. Yet the depression did not engender a serious threat to the system. The morale of the northern working class was sustained through years of material hardship by a way of life which had been long established by the 1930s. For many men the focal point of this culture was the working man's club. The Club and Institute Union amalgamated a great variety of organisations. Some were political: Conservative, Liberal and, increasingly, Labour. Others were friendly societies, like the Oddfellows or the Royal Antediluvian Order of Buffaloes. The benefits which these conferred on members, such as sickness and burial schemes, were particularly attractive inducements to join in the period before the full establishment of the welfare state. But the main attraction was the entertainment which they provided. This did not just consist of drinking at prices and at times more relaxed than those which obtained in the public houses, though such concessions as beer at two-thirds the price of a pint in the pub could not be lightly dismissed, especially during a depression. Billiards and snooker, darts and dominoes were available every night. And at least once a week there would be the 'turn', when an entertainer, such as a singer or a comedian, would perform in the concert or music room, the last survivors of the music-halls which had flourished at the turn of the century. On these weekly occasions, as a special concession, women were allowed to accompany the all-male members. Otherwise the functions of the working man's club catered for that sex alone. The alternative for women was to go to the cinema at least once and often twice a week. During the winter they might accompany men to a football game, either soccer or rugby league, though the notion that these once catered for whole families until hooliganism drove women and children away in the 1970s is something of a myth. There has never been the level of violence at rugby league games which can accompany soccer matches, yet the crowds who go to watch them have always consisted overwhelmingly of young adult males.

There are those who regard such leisure activities as the modern equivalent of the provision of bread and circuses by Roman emperors to maintain social control. To explain working-class culture in terms of a bourgeois conspiracy to maintain class hegemony, however, is to indulge in enormous condescension. The clubs, the cinemas and the football grounds provided more than a mere means of escape from a bleak existence or a diversion from political activity. Had material considerations been a priority for the working class, then they might well have saved the money spent on leisure activities to purchase goods and services. Many chose to spend on short-term pleasure even at the expense of long-term benefits such as annual outings to the seaside. They spent more money on the remote long-term benefit of winning on the football pools than they put into savings accounts. And had politics been a priority, then they would have channelled their energies into political activities. In fact politics and politicians seemed very remote to most of them. Depression and unemployment seemed like inescapable facts of life to the majority rather than problems admitting of a political solution. What was real was the experience of them shared with neighbours and workmates, the people with whom they shared their pleasures too. It was a gregarious way of life. Radio only partially began to isolate families in their homes. The last generation to live before the advent of television and videos thought of entertainment as a collective rather than as a solitary activity. The comedians who made them laugh in their clubs or on the 'wireless' knew more about genuine working-class values than any politicians. And their humour tended to reinforce conservative and even reactionary prejudices rather than to inculcate radicalism.

The outbreak of the Second World War found the working class in better physical and perhaps psychological state than had been the case in the summer of 1914. Only a third of the recruits were unacceptable on grounds of fitness compared with twice that proportion twenty-five years earlier. Better housing as well as a better diet were mainly responsible for this improvement. Between the wars local authorities built one and a half million houses for rent, most of them replacing former slums. In 1939 conscription was introduced immediately, so there was no reliance on the jingoist hysteria which had whipped up military passions against the Kaiser. At the same time men were readier to accept the need to contain Hitler's aggressive ambitions in Europe, so that fewer objected on conscientious grounds to the introduction of compulsory military service, while their objections were more sympathetically received than in the earlier conflict.

The experience of the Second World War changed working-class attitudes towards politics to a significant extent. Where the Great War had seemed a monstrous aberration from the norm, a nightmare from which men woke up in 1918, the later conflict was seen as a deliberate act to purge the world of fascism. After the armistice most people appear to have wanted as far as possible to restore the civilisation which had been destroyed in the trenches. In 1945 few wanted to turn the clock back to 1939. A sea change had taken place in the collective consciousness. The proposition that politicians could actually influence everyday life for better or for worse was much more widely accepted at all levels of society.

These changing attitudes were possibly due, in part at least, to the fact that during the war the state affected the lives of people to such an extent that they became accustomed to its role. Identity cards were introduced for everybody with the national registration of all British subjects, a move which had been successfully resisted in the First World War. Landlords at the top of society found that their houses and estates could be requisitioned for the war effort. Many country houses were appropriated by the government while over half a million acres of land were acquired for military purposes. All classes were subject to rationing, but perhaps the middle class felt its purchasing power to be most restricted by it. Food rationing had been introduced in 1917, but had not been as effectively enforced. Now clothes as well as food were rationed soon after war broke out. Although a black market came into operation it did not lead to widespread evasion of the rationing system until after the war ended. Although ration books were still being issued as late as 1952 there can be little doubt that by then there was general reluctance to abide by the regulations. In the late 1940s the 'spivs and drones' who defied the food office inspectorate were regarded as figures of fun rather than as public enemies.

One of the effects of wartime rationing was to improve the general standard of nutrition. Children in particular benefited from the scarcity of sugar, their teeth requiring far less attention than their parents' had done. But the whole population had a more balanced diet than had prevailed in the twenties and thirties, even if some fruits, such as bananas, disappeared from greengrocers' shelves for the duration. Expectant mothers were provided with free milk and orange juice. Clothes coupons also paradoxically meant that relatively more was spent on clothing than had been the case previously. Working-class families were better fed and dressed at the end of the war than they had been at the beginning, when the condition of children evacuated from the East End of London to the provinces had shocked their hosts.

In the early stages of the war over a million children were evacuated, most of them from working-class districts felt to be particularly vulnerable to air raids. The government organised their transportation, but left their reception to local authorities. Since those responsible for transportation anticipated a much bigger response they laid on too many trains, and despatched children in trainloads as they arrived without reference to the arrangements made to receive them. The result was administrative chaos, which did not get the scheme off to a good start.

The experience of evacuation was not a particularly happy one

21   Evacuation of London schoolchildren, June 1940

either. The evacuees themselves were bewildered and even frightened by their transition from familiar working-class streets to strange cities and even stranger villages. Their hosts were often appalled to find their guests harboured lice in their hair or wet their beds. Many evacuees returned, especially from the first wave in 1939 which took place during the 'phoney war' before air raids started in earnest. Others, such as those from the Channel Islands, had no choice but to stay for the duration of the war.

When the 'blitz' began it brought civilians into the front line of a war for the first time. While London took the brunt of the air raids attacks were by no means confined to the capital or the south of England. Hull was the second most frequently bombed city, while Clydeside was not spared. The raids in fact threatened the urban populations of the whole country. Where during the First World War civilian casualties were negligible, between 1940 and 1945 60,000 were killed by enemy action, one-fifth of the total number of those who died in the armed forces. In the first two years of the war the enemy killed more civilians than soldiers, sailors or airmen. Thereafter the air raids became far less frequent, producing a lull which was terrifyingly ended with the V1 pilotless planes, or 'doodlebugs', and V2 rocket attacks of the last year of the war. The German air force hoped by these raids to sap civilian morale to the point of creating public demands for the ending of the conflict. In fact the reverse seems to have been the case, the raids provoking a stiffening of the will to resist.

Indeed to dwell on the privations of the 'home front' as it was called is to miss an important aspect of these years. For the war undoubtedly brought benefits as well as losses. One of them was full employment. As late as 1940 there were still a million unemployed. By 1943 the shortage of labour was so serious that the virtual conscription of women for war work, introduced in 1941, was extended to include those between eighteen and fifty. During the war something like 2 million women were added to the workforce. Labour shortages led to wage increases, real wages rising on average by 9 per cent between 1938 and 1945. Moreover 'overtime' and bonus payments gave workers on munitions something nearer a 20 per cent increase.

There was a marked fear that these improved living standards would not be sustained after the war, when troops were demobilised on to the labour market. At the same time there was a commitment to maintaining full employment. One solution to this problem was to persuade women to give up their jobs and to return to domesticity. The propaganda was so successful that many women did leave their wartime employment in order to have children and raise families. So far from there being a surplus of workers, however, the post-war years actually witnessed a severe labour shortage. Attempts to throw the propaganda into reverse and attract women back into industry were on the whole unsuccessful, not least because the state failed to provide creches for working women. Consequently sources of labour were sought elsewhere, not least in the Commonwealth, where workers in the West Indies and in the Indian subcontinent were recruited to jobs in Britain. They performed much needed tasks as doctors and nurses in the health service, bus drivers in local authority transport, and labourers in woollen mills.

The numbers of immigrants who came were not overwhelming. Indeed Britain lost more by emigration than she gained through immigration during the 1950s and 1960s. Nevertheless the nature of the influx differed markedly from previous patterns of immigration, such as that which after the Second World War had brought Eastern

Europeans to Britain. To be sure there were cultural and linguistic differences between the immigrants and the host communities in the late 1940s, and much prejudice was voiced against the 'displaced peoples' as those who came from the Baltic states overrun by the Soviet Union were called. 'Deport the DPs' had appeared as a slogan on walls at the time. But being Christians and Europeans they were quickly absorbed into British society. It was the ethnicity of the new arrivals which made such absorption difficult for West Indians and Asians. They discovered a strong streak of racial prejudice in the 'mother country'. In the case of peoples from Pakistan this was aggravated by the fact that they were Moslems and spoke Urdu. Moreover they did not spread out through society but concentrated in particular cities such as Birmingham and Bradford. Communities which had been remarkably homogeneous for generations suddenly found themselves becoming multi-racial societies. The rapidity of the change was a shock to the social system. For example corner shops which had been a focus of local life, selling beer, cigarettes, milk, tea and other familiar goods changed hands and began to stock rice, spices and other 'alien' commodities. The process generated fear and resentment and fuelled demands for strict controls on further immigration. The more ignorant fantasies were exploited by unscrupulous politicians to campaign for repatriation. It was this issue above all which led extreme right wing organisations to combine into the National Front in 1966. Yet this party failed to attract more than a tiny minority of supporters. The fragile consensus was maintained by the major parties. Conservative and Labour governments passed acts in 1962, 1965 and 1968 to curtail further immigration, while at the same time attempts were made to prevent race becoming a political issue. Thus an Institute of Race Relations was set up in 1958 to be followed by the establishment of the Race Relations Board in 1966, while discrimination in employment and housing was made illegal in 1968.

The ability of Britain to absorb these strains and to become a genuinely multi-racial society depended to a large extent upon the state of the economy. As long as full employment was sustained, and there was no severe competition for jobs, then racial conflict could be kept in check. From this point of view conditions were better after the Second World War than they had been before. At no time between 1922 and 1939 was the number of registered unemployed lower than a million, and in 1932 it peaked at 2,745,000. At no time between 1945 and 1975 did it reach a million, and for most of that period it was below 500,000, though from 1967 onwards the trend was upward, and in 1976 it went above a million for the first time since 1939.

Of course aggregate statistics conceal regional differences. The pre-war pattern of unemployment affecting the regions where the traditional industries of coal, steel and textiles were located was reproduced after 1945, and any recession affected them more severely than the midlands and the south-east of England. It was also becoming clear by the 1960s that Britain's newer industries producing motor vehicles and electrical goods were suffering from foreign competition, and that services like supermarkets and tourism were more buoyant sectors of the economy. Some faith was placed in the prospect that a new technological revolution based on electronics would come to Britain's rescue, but somehow this never materialised.

Economically indeed Britain appeared to be in terminal decline. As Britons showed their preference for imported consumer goods over domestic products so the balance of payments became an ever more serious problem, current account moving into deficits redeemed only by 'invisible' earnings from shipping, insurance and other financial services in the City. In order to cope with this problem governments of both major parties curtailed demand by tightening credit facilities. This produced a slow-down in the economy which, it was piously hoped, manufacturers would use to build up supplies of improved products which would corner the domestic market when the squeeze was relaxed. Unfortunately this never happened, and when the relaxation occurred imports were sucked in to satisfy consumer demand. The result was a wearisome cycle of 'stop-go' interventions by government in the economy. It seemed as though there was no political solution to the underlying economic decline. Devaluation of the pound, and letting it 'float' against other currencies, were both tried, but neither proved to be more than a temporary expedient. Import controls were suggested, but no party was prepared to implement them in case of reprisals from overseas competitors.

It was against this gloomy background that membership of the European Economic Community began to appear more and more attractive. The British government's first tentative approach to the community, in 1961, was rebuffed by France. Another attempt in 1967

EUROPE'S BIGGEST DAILY SALE

3p   Monday, January 1, 1973   ✦   ✦   ✦   No. 21,449

JANUARY 1, 1973

A DAY IN HISTORY

GREAT BRITAIN goes into GREATER EUROPE

What does it mean to YOU? Please turn to Page 2

22   Britain joins the EEC: front page of the *Daily Mirror*, 1
January 1973

was also abortive. But the third application was successful, and Britain
joined the EEC in 1973. The notion that membership would cure
economic decline was not without its critics. Those on the right tended
to stress the advantages of trade within the British Commonwealth.
This argument, however, became less and less compelling as Britain
retreated from its imperial commitments while Canada and New
Zealand ceased to be major trading partners. Voices on both the right
and the left of British politics objected to the surrender of sovereignty,

which would mean the end of a thousand years of history. Those on the left tended to suspect the Common Market as a capitalist club, and feared that state control of the British economy would prove unfeasible if sovereignty were surrendered. When a Labour government took office in 1974, therefore, it insisted upon a referendum on the question of British membership. The results, in 1975, showed that two-thirds of those who voted were in favour. It might not have signalled the end of a thousand years of history, but it certainly marked the start of a new era.

7

From the Boer War to the first Labour government

The years of the Boer War saw the Liberals divided and the Conservatives and Liberal Unionists united, while in the run up to the 1906 election these roles were reversed. The Unionists fell apart over education and tariff reform, measures which healed the divisions in the Liberal ranks.

Although Chamberlain sneered at the Liberals as being pro-Boer many supported the war, including a former prime minister, Rosebery, and a future premier, Asquith. There were rival dinner parties hosted by the two groups, which one wit satirised as 'war to the knife and fork'. With the ending of hostilities, however, these divisions largely disappeared.

In 1902 an Education Act sponsored by A. J. Balfour alienated nonconformists and with them many of the government's Liberal Unionist supporters. It abolished the school boards and put secondary schooling under local education authorities, including Anglican schools which became rate supported. The hostile reaction of other Protestant denominations was to be expected. The conversion of a former Liberal to tariff reform, however, was not so predictable. Joseph Chamberlain came out strongly in favour of it as a solution to the problems besetting British industry from foreign competition. Although as colonial secretary he had become convinced of the advantages of imperial preference to protect trade before his advocacy of it at Birmingham in May 1903, his speech was regarded as a major challenge to the prevailing ideology of free trade. The challenge was taken up by Balfour, who had succeeded Salisbury as prime minister and saw it as a threat to his leadership. Chamberlain resigned from the cabinet in September to take the debate to the country. He calculated that a general election would be held on the issue shortly afterwards. In fact Balfour clung on to office for another two years, and when he did finally resign he advised the king to appoint a Liberal government rather than dissolve parliament.

Sir Henry Campbell-Bannerman was thereupon asked to form an administration. His cabinet was one of the more impressive of the twentieth century, including Asquith as chancellor, Sir Edward Grey as foreign secretary and Lloyd George as president of the board of trade. Winston Churchill, who had just left the Conservatives over tariff reform, also became a minister as under-secretary for the colonies. Almost immediately after taking office the new prime minister requested a dissolution.

The general election of 1906 was a watershed in British political history. By-election trends predicted a Liberal victory on the scale of 1885. In the event they did rather less well in terms of votes cast, polling 54 per cent at the first and only 49 per cent at the second. But the distorting effect of single-member constituencies and 'first past the post' voting worked more in their favour in 1906, for they obtained 400 seats then compared with only 335 in 1885. They might have taken more if the Labour Representation Committee had not emerged to field its own candidates. To avert three-cornered contests which would benefit the Unionists the Liberal whip Herbert Gladstone did a deal with Ramsay MacDonald, the secretary of the LRC, in which they agreed as far as possible not to set up rival candidates in the same constituencies. Although they denied such a pact in public it was remarkably successful in practice. Outside London there was only one constituency where a candidate backed by the LRC opposed a Liberal. Thirty LRC candidates were returned. On arrival at Westminster they called themselves the Labour party and took their seats on the opposition benches.

Herbert Gladstone has been accused of letting a Trojan horse into the Commons, one which would eventually produce enough MPs to replace the Liberals as the party of the left. The decline of the Liberal party has been exhaustively diagnosed, but to date it from the moment of its greatest triumph seems a little perverse. It is true that they did not need an electoral pact to get control of the Commons. Their own members constituted an overall majority, with the Conservatives and Liberal Unionists in disarray over tariff reform and having between them only 157 seats, despite polling over 43 per cent of votes cast. Yet Gladstone was clearly seeking to maximise the anti-Unionist vote. Where 153 Unionists had been returned unopposed at the previous general election only five were given a clear field at this. In fielding candidates against them Gladstone took pains to avoid three-cornered contests not only with the LRC but also with the so-called Lib-Labs, only four of whom fought in constituencies where Liberals also stood. He deserves the credit for creating an electoral machine which did as much to ensure the Unionists' humiliating defeat as it did his own party's landslide victory.

Insofar as issues rather than organisation swung the electorate, overwhelmingly the advocates of free trade overcame those in favour of tariff reform. Both aimed their appeal not only at the voters in general but at the labour vote in particular. Protectionists argued that tariffs were necessary to protect jobs as well as profits. Free traders urged that protection would increase prices of basic foodstuffs: 'If you want your loaf, you must shut up Joe.' Unionists also tried to raise the spectre of home rule in an attempt to throw their opponents into disarray, but the Liberals failed to oblige them. They renewed their pledge to it, but declined to give it priority in their programme. Apart from advocating free trade they appealed to the nonconformist and working-class voters. Nonconformists were offered amendments to the Education Act, while workers were wooed with commitments to poor law reform, pensions and trade union law.

How far these appeals were effective is difficult to discern, since the swing was so great and, outside the midlands where Chamberlain held his own, so uniform. The Unionists lost the cities and the counties. Workers might have voted more enthusiastically for working-class candidates, the swing against the Unionists being highest in seats where they were opposed by the LRC. But they polled substantially for Liberals too. The notion that the Liberal party was losing its grass roots support with the rise of Labour is difficult to sustain in the light of the 1906 results.

The years 1906 to 1910 marked a crucial change in the ideological context of British politics. At the general election of 1906 religion still set the main political agenda and probably influenced the behaviour of most voters. It is significant that the Liberal ranks returned to Westminster contained 157 out of a total of 185 nonconformist MPs, the largest number ever elected. By the elections of 1910 class had replaced religion as the main dynamic of electoral politics. The polarisation of the electorate along class lines was to remain a salient feature of the political scene in the twentieth century.

To a large extent this realignment came about as a result of the Liberals' resolve to use their large majority in the Commons to achieve substantial reforms and the determination of their opponents to use their control of the upper House to frustrate them. 'The people versus the peers' thus became the overriding political issue.

The primacy of religious issues in 1906 was illustrated by the first arenas in which the two Houses fought, education and licensing. An education bill was introduced in the first session of the new parliament which sought to amend Balfour's act by placing the maintained schools firmly in the management of local authorities who were to take no notice of their religious affiliations, for example by requiring teachers to subscribe to them. The king expressed concern about this measure to the Archbishop of Canterbury, objecting that it would 'produce violent dissensions between the Church of England and Roman Catholics on one side and the nonconformists on the other...a kind of political-religious warfare...which is most undesirable'. Though the bill passed the Commons with overwhelming backing the peers piled on amendments which virtually nullified it. There resulted a head-on clash in which the lower House rejected the amendments *unanimously* while the upper House insisted on them. The government was obliged to drop the bill, much to the chagrin of the nonconformists.

Nonconformity also endorsed the Licensing Bill of 1908 which sought to reduce the number of licensed premises by about a third over a period of fourteen years. It was perhaps ironic that this temperance measure should be vigorously pressed by Asquith, whose own drinking habits were so notorious that they introduced a new word into the language: 'squiffy'. Again it was voted through its second and third readings in the Commons by huge majorities, only to be defeated by the Lords. On its rejection Winston Churchill observed, 'They have started the class war.'

Churchill was by then president of the board of trade, a new cabinet having been formed by Asquith, who became prime minister on the death of Campbell-Bannerman. Lloyd George succeeded Asquith as chancellor of the exchequer. In 1909 he introduced the so-called 'People's Budget' which threw down the gauntlet to the peers. It sought to raise revenue partly by indirect taxes on such items as motor cars and petrol, but mainly by direct taxes on incomes, land and licenses and by death duties. Most of the incidence fell on the wealthy. The Lords accused the Liberals of wishing to 'soak the rich'.

Others have ascribed the thinking behind the budget to more elevated principles. It has been seen as a major contribution to what was dubbed the 'new liberalism'. Where under Gladstone the Liberal party stood for economy, retrenchment and *laisser-faire*, by the turn of the nineteenth century Liberal thought, stimulated by academic theorists, had come to accept the state's intervention to alleviate social conditions by fiscal policy. Thus Asquith had budgeted for old age pensions when he was chancellor of the exchequer. Single persons over seventy with incomes of less than £26 were to get five shillings a week; married couples seven shillings and sixpence. Part of Lloyd George's problems arose from the fact that his predecessor had underestimated the sums required, while more generous provision increased them too. Thus the distinction between single and married persons was eliminated.

One of the difficulties facing any Edwardian chancellor was that state expenditure was rising rapidly. Where in 1895 it amounted to £156,800,000, by 1913 it had risen to £305,400,000. Much of this was spent on defence. Lloyd George needed money for eight Dreadnought battleships as well as for old age pensions. The key to Edwardian politics was how to raise these sums. The Unionists put forward the solution of tariff reform. The Liberals sought it while retaining free trade. Increases of taxation were regarded by both as inevitable. The principle of old age pensions was not attacked by the Unionists. But the recourse to direct levies on those held to be most able to pay was associated with the Liberals rather than with their rivals. Lloyd George in an unguarded moment had actually said 'I have got to rob somebody's hen roost.' He was determined not to rob middle-class Liberal voters. So the Lords were right to conclude that his budget strategy was deliberately designed to hit those like themselves who were natural supporters of the Unionist cause.

This partisan element in the budget determined the Unionists to oppose it at every stage. It was introduced by Lloyd George in a four-hour speech on 29 April, and finally passed the Commons on 4 November after 554 divisions. On 30 November it was defeated in the Lords by 350 votes to 75.

The rejection of the government's finance bill caused a major constitutional and political crisis. It had been established for over two centuries that the Lords could not amend a money bill, but could only pass or reject it. The upper House had, however, objected to 'tacking' proposals to money bills which had nothing to do with finance in order to force them through the Lords, and had threatened to reject any such measure. On this occasion it was claimed that the extra cost of liquor licenses was a 'tack' since the Lords had rejected the Licensing Bill in the previous session. The Commons claimed that its mandate from the electorate overrode any other constitutional consideration, including the Lords' claim to be able to reject money bills, which should be dropped as anachronistic.

More to the point was the political argument that the Lords only used their power to reject bills passed by the Commons when the government of the day was Liberal. They docilely acquiesced in measures promoted by Conservative ministries. This led Lloyd George to criticise the Lords as 'Mr Balfour's poodle'. He also inveighed against the class as well as the partisan nature of the confrontation in two notorious speeches at Limehouse and Newcastle. The Limehouse speech in July led the king to complain that it could only have the effect of setting class against class. The Newcastle speech in October was even more radical. 'Who made ten thousand people owners of the soil' he asked, 'and the rest of us trespassers in the land of our birth? Let them realise what they are doing. They are forcing a revolution.'

They were not so much forcing a revolution as a general election on the issue of the peers versus the people. One was promptly held in January 1910. It produced a turn-out of 87 per cent, the highest of any this century. Even allowing for the freshness of the electoral registers this was still a testimony to the high interest aroused by the issues involved. The Unionists polled 3,127,887 votes and obtained 273 seats, the Liberals polled 2,880,581 votes and gained 275 seats. Once again the distorting effect of the 1885 Redistribution Act manifested itself, with one party getting 46.9 per cent of the votes cast and winning only 40.7 per cent of the seats while another got 43.2 per cent of the votes and 41 per cent of the seats. Labour candidates polled 7.6 per cent of the votes and obtained forty seats, 5.9 per cent of the total. The Liberals would now be dependent upon their support and that of the eighty-two Irish Nationalists where before they had had an overall majority.

These results reflected a 4.3 per cent 'swing' to the Unionists since 1906. But the swing was by no means evenly distributed throughout the country. In Scotland it was only 1.8 per cent, in Wales 1.9 per cent, and in the north 3.0 per cent, whereas in the home counties it was more like 8.0 per cent. Beatrice Webb analysed the outcome in terms endorsed by modern investigators. 'What is remarkable is the dividing of England into two distinct halves each having its own large majority for its own cause – the south country, the suburban, agricultural residential England going Tory ... and the north country and dense industrial populations (excluding Birmingham) going Radical-Socialist.' As the historian of the 1910 elections concludes, the Unionists had done well in the south and the Liberals in the Celtic fringe and the north before, but never so well at the same election. 'In the north, Scotland and Wales the Liberal position was slightly eroded; in the south it was washed away in the tide of Unionist reaction.' The social implications of this electoral geography are striking. The new liberalism appealed to the industrial working men, but alienated the suburban middle classes even though Lloyd George had sought to protect them from the impact of his budget. As he himself admitted in September 1909, 'I believe the budget has secured the enthusiasm of the vast majority of the working men of the kingdom; but it is nonconformity alone that can bring the middle classes to our aid.' Unfortunately for the Liberals class had replaced religion as the electoral touchstone, a transformation which they had done much to effect.

Though the Liberals were disappointed with the outcome of the January elections it confirmed their stance against the peers on the issue of the budget, which was passed by the new parliament. However, the question of the powers of the House of Lords remained unresolved. After their defeat of the Education Bill plans had been formulated to curb the veto of the upper House, but these had been abortive. In 1911 they were revived in the Parliament Bill, which deprived the Lords of their right to reject financial measures altogether, and only allowed them to delay other legislation which had the support of a Commons majority for two years. It passed through the lower House by the end of April, but before it could be debated by the Lords the king's death temporarily postponed debates on the issue.

The first few months of George V's reign were spent in efforts to resolve the deadlock. A constitutional convention was held where the positions of the two Houses were rehearsed with a view to finding a compromise. At one stage Lloyd George even recommended a coalition government, on the basis of the Liberals and Unionists moderating partisan measures likely to create friction between the two Houses. But the issue of home rule was one on which no compromise was possible. The discussions ended when the Liberals refused to agree to submit such issues to a referendum if the peers blocked them. Instead they asked the king for a dissolution, and for the creation of enough peers to pass the Parliament Bill should that become necessary.

The results of the general election held in December 1910 almost exactly reproduced those of the contest which had taken place at the beginning of the year. Once again the Unionists polled more votes than the Liberals, 3,127,887 against 2,880,581, but gained only the same number of seats, 272. Labour and Irish Nationalists each obtained two seats more than they had done in January. The fact that there was a lower turn-out while fewer seats were contested has led some observers to conclude that the electorate was bored with the business of 'peers versus people'. However, the fall in the proportion of the electorate polling was almost entirely due to the staleness of the electoral registers, and the drop in the incidence of contests was attributable to the political parties deciding to cut their losses fighting seats which had been won overwhelmingly by their rivals only a few months earlier. The most striking outcome of the second election was the confirmation of the geographical and social division of the country between the Liberals and their allies on the one hand and the Unionists on the other.

The government could now claim that it had a mandate for the Parliament Bill. As it progressed towards the statute book the Conservative peers came to realise that the king was prepared, however reluctantly, to ennoble enough men to force it through their House. Though some opposed it notwithstanding, others lost their nerve and either abstained or even voted for the bill as it made its way through the Lords in August 1911 during a heatwave which registered the highest temperatures of the century before 1990.

The year 1911 marked the peak of the reforming zeal of the last

Liberal government. Apart from the Parliament Act the most important measure was the National Insurance Act. Lloyd George was primarily responsible for this scheme which sought to insure workers in some industries against unemployment and manual workers in general against sickness. Unemployment benefits aroused little criticism, but health insurance ran into opposition from the medical profession, friendly societies and insurance companies, and even from workers themselves who objected to the weekly contributions being deducted from their wage packets. Lloyd George rode out the storm of protest, buying off the private health schemes by including them in the administrative machinery. The National Insurance Act remained his most enduring monument, so that even today old people refer to getting a sick note as 'going on the Lloyd George'.

Further social legislation, such as a land reform measure, was planned, but the momentum for reform ran into the sands of home rule, which occupied the bulk of parliamentary time in the next three sessions. The Liberals had managed to avoid this contentious issue between 1906 and 1910, when they had an overall majority. Now that they were dependent upon Irish Nationalist support in the Commons something had to be done about the government of Ireland. That something, however, was equally inevitably bound to run into Unionist opposition, especially in the Lords. The Parliament Act provided the ministers with the means of getting round that resistance, but only after two years had passed. The result was that a Home Rule Bill had to pass the Commons three times, and did not reach the statute book until September 1914, only to become a dead letter because of the outbreak of war.

Although Unionist intransigence was predictable, the form it took was not. Or at least the government did not predict it, since they made no provision for Ulster in the original bill; yet the fate of the Protestant north-east became the main bone of contention between the parties. The Unionists, led by Bonar Law after Balfour's resignation as party leader, took up the Orange cause literally with a vengeance. The cries 'Ulster will fight and Ulster will be right' and 'Home Rule is Rome Rule' were revived. Bonar Law was even reported as saying to a huge public gathering at Blenheim Palace in July 1912 'I can imagine no length of resistance to which Ulster will go in which I shall not be ready to support them.'

Where the cause of Ulster united the Unionists it divided the Liberals. It was in fact a Liberal, Agar-Robarts, who introduced an amendment to exempt four northern counties from the provisions of the bill. Though his amendment was defeated there were sixty-two government abstentions on the division, while five Liberals voted for it. The main source of the unease over Ulster in Liberal ranks was nonconformity, since the nonconformists in Britain, especially in Scotland and Wales, were apprehensive for the fate of the Presbyterians in Northern Ireland under a Dublin government.

Conservative opposition in the Lords kept the issue before parliament until 1914. Meanwhile contingent plans were made in Ulster by Sir Edward Carson and his supporters to resist the implementation of the measure should it ever become an act. On 28 September a Solemn League and Covenant was signed by hundreds of thousands of Ulstermen, some, it was said, in blood. Almost as many women signed a similar document. Volunteers were drilled at first without arms but eventually with weapons smuggled in from Germany. It seemed that civil war was becoming unavoidable in Ireland. The government too took military and naval precautions to prevent this but these partly backfired in 1914 when officers stationed at the Curragh resigned rather than face the prospect of suppressing an uprising in the north.

To some rebellion seemed likely in Britain as well as in Ireland. According to Claud Cockburn in the years immediately preceding the outbreak of war in 1914 his family used to discuss which would come first, that or the revolution. Militancy in the Labour movement seemed to be directing it into extra-parliamentary activity to achieve its ends. Certainly there were grounds for disillusionment with the performance of Labour MPs. So far from making inroads into the existing system they seemed to have been contained and even repulsed by it. In 1910 forty took their seats after the first election and forty-two at the second. Almost all owed their returns to the agreement of Liberals not to oppose them. Between 1910 and 1914 the trend in by-elections, some of which saw three-cornered fights, actually reduced their ranks to thirty-six. The Liberals seemed to be stealing their clothes with the provision of old age pensions and national insurance. The only achievement which the Labour members could claim the credit for during these years was the reversal of the Osborne judgment of 1909, which had hit party funds hard by making the political levy from trade union funds illegal. The Liberals removed this obstacle to electoral activity in 1913.

There were two reactions to the Osborne judgment. One was to close ranks with the Labour party. Thus the miners affiliated in 1909 and ended the separate existence of 'Lib-Lab' MPs, who now joined other Labour members. Another was to seek solutions to labour disputes in strikes rather than in votes. In 1912 the miners and the dockers went on strike. 1913 witnessed the largest number of stoppages for any year before the outbreak of the First World War. Some of these strikes were influenced by syndicalist thinking. Syndicalism repudiated parliamentary solutions to labour problems and sought instead to use organised union activity to achieve its ends. This resort to direct action seemed to threaten parliament itself. In response to it the *Sunday Times* claimed in January 1912 that 'we are within measurable distance of civil war'.

It was at this time too that the suffragette movement became more militant. In 1913 Emily Davison achieved immortality by throwing herself under the king's horse at the Derby, while Emmeline Pankhurst went to prison for causing a bomb to be exploded in a house under construction for Lloyd George, who ironically was in favour of votes for women. Suffragettes sent to prison went on hunger strike and were subjected to the dreadful ordeal of forcible feeding. Such treatment put any government, especially one claiming radical credentials, in an unfavourable light. To try to avoid the unfavourable publicity the ministers put a so-called 'Cat and Mouse' Act on the statute book, which provided for the release of hunger strikers from gaol until they were fit enough to be imprisoned again.

The difficulties faced by the Liberal government in dealing with the crises presented by the intransigence of the House of Lords, the agitation over Ulster, and militancy in the labour and suffragette movements have been seen as a failure of liberalism itself. A political philosophy which assumed that the tensions between the individual and society could be resolved by achieving a consensus in representative institutions was allegedly perplexed by the manifest failure of the system to achieve the result. The parliamentary machinery itself had broken down in the clash between the two Houses. The sovereignty of parliament was being attacked by Ulstermen, trades unionists and feminists. The very fabric of society seemed to be tearing apart. Only

23 'The shrieking sister'; a satirical view of the suffragettes

the assertion of the authority of the state, itself anathema to a creed of *laisser-faire* and non-intervention, could stop the rot.

Yet this is to exaggerate the degree to which 'Liberal England' was undergoing its death throes on the eve of the First World War. For one thing the threats posed by militancy were becoming less rather than more serious, in Britain at least. The number of stoppages in industry dropped sharply in 1914. The violence of the suffragette movement was counter-productive. The very resort to it was due to desperation at the failure of persuasion to convert politicians or the general public, while the breaking of store windows and the arson attacks on property alienated the majority of women let alone men from the cause. Only the Irish problem was becoming more and more insoluble, but Ireland has always been regarded even by radical politicians as a special case to which the normal rules of the game do not apply. Besides, the rules were changing. The 'new' liberalism had come a long way from the individualism and *laisser-faire* of Victorian days. So far from flinching from using the state to solve society's problems Asquith's cabinet resorted to it willingly. It was the war which dealt the death blow to Edwardian liberalism. Ironically the industrial unrest and suffragette militancy, allegedly so fatal to it, receded as trade unionists agreed to support the war effort, while the suffragettes suspended their activities for the duration. But the unprecedented needs of total warfare made necessary measures which had been anathema to Liberals. The very declaration of war by a Liberal cabinet was a controversial decision from a party which had voiced criticism of wars in general and the Boer War in particular. Only the conviction that they retained the high moral ground against Germany after the invasion of Belgium held the ministry together. The Defence of the Realm Act passed in August 1914 set up a censorship to restrict reporting of the war. The budget of 1915 introduced duties on 'luxury' imports and marked the end of free trade. 'So the old system goes,' remarked Lloyd George in cabinet. And in January 1916 compulsory military service was imposed on unmarried men aged between eighteen and forty-one.

The tension between sacrificing principle to win the war and saving the Liberal soul came to be personified in the struggle between Lloyd George and Asquith. Asquith himself made the first move in the duel when, for reasons which have never been satisfactorily explained, he formed a coalition with the Conservatives in May 1915. The most plausible explanation is that the Parliament Act of 1911 had shortened the maximum interval between general elections from seven to five years. In the normal course of events, therefore, one was due in 1915. A dissolution of parliament was regarded as unwise during the war, but could only be avoided with the consent of the Conservatives, given their majority in the Lords. At all events Asquith made room in the cabinet for leading Conservatives, and even gave a ministerial post to the Labour leader Arthur Henderson. At the same time he took the opportunity to move Lloyd George from the chancellorship of the exchequer to the newly created post of minister of munitions. Possibly he hoped that his emerging rival would be exposed to merciless criticism in the press which had mounted a campaign against an alleged shortage of shells at the front. In fact he made the new ministry a powerhouse of production. So far from the press baying for his blood, he won it to his side in the final rounds of his fight against Asquith.

At the start of 1916 both Lloyd George and Asquith thought that the business of winning the war was best left to the generals. Lloyd George pinned his faith in General Haig's strategy of breaking through the enemy lines with a massive effort. But when this was tried at the Somme that summer and autumn it produced horrific casualty figures with no signs of a breakthrough. At the end of the year Lloyd George got Conservative support for a challenge to Asquith's leadership which took the form of a demand that a small council chaired by himself should be set up to direct the war effort. Asquith at first agreed but then, backed up by influential Liberals, withdrew his agreement. Lloyd George thereupon resigned. His resignation was followed the next day by Asquith's own. It was a strange decision, perhaps unduly influenced by his mental state following the death of his son in battle. Apparently he hoped that neither the Conservative leader Bonar Law nor Lloyd George would be able to form a government. He was right as far as Bonar Law was concerned, for when the king sent for him he made it a condition that Asquith should serve, which the former prime minister refused. But Lloyd George was prepared to succeed him, and took office at the head of a new coalition. Asquith promptly became leader of the opposition, thus splitting the Liberal party between his own supporters and those who supported the government. On the whole the coalitionists were on the Liberal right while the

24   Lloyd George and Churchill, 1915

Asquithians were on the left. Many of the latter later joined the Labour party.

At the time Labour officially supported the coalition. Henderson was a minister without portfolio in Lloyd George's war cabinet which had only five members. The Labour leader resigned in 1917 in order to attend an international socialist meeting in Stockholm, but although his colleagues disapproved of his attendance he was replaced in the cabinet by G. N. Barnes. Henderson's resignation boosted the influence of Labour members such as Ramsay MacDonald and Philip Snowden who had stood out against the war. This division between pro- and anti-war sections of the Labour movement had reached its height in 1915, when on the death of Keir Hardie candidates representing both positions contested his vacant seat. Not surprisingly the pro-war candidate won easily. On Henderson's departure from the government he worked hard to heal this breach in the Labour party. He also promoted its transformation from a pressure group into a genuine national party prepared to take power. Thus Henderson played a major part in the adoption of a new constitution in 1918, which committed the Labour party to setting up an organisation in every constituency as well as to socialist objectives.

The only party which emphatically refused to support either the Asquith or the Lloyd George coalition was the Irish Nationalists. Their goal of home rule, already deferred for the duration of the war, was further jeopardised by the advent of Unionists to office. Bonar Law was colonial secretary in the first coalition and chancellor of the exchequer in the second, while Carson became attorney general. John Redmond, the Nationalist leader, was offered a post but declined.

Frustration at the deferment of home rule fed the aspirations of those who wished for complete independence. At Easter 1916 a band of republicans seized public buildings in Dublin and held them for four days, during which 450 people were killed and 2,600 wounded. After the suppression of the rebellion fifteen rebels were hanged and thousands were imprisoned. These reprisals can be attributed to the nervousness of the British government that the Germans would use Ireland as a back door. One of the conspirators was landed near Dublin by a German submarine. The Irish outside Ulster showed a disinclination to become involved in the war as an abortive attempt to extend conscription to Ireland revealed. Yet, however understandable the reaction might be, it spelled the end of the Union. The rebels became martyrs. A convention set up to resolve the problem of home rule was inconclusive. At the general election of 1918, Sinn Fein ('ourselves alone') swept to victory at the polls, winning seventy-three seats to the Nationalists' seven. They refused to attend the Westminster parliament and convened their own in Dublin instead.

In Britain coalition candidates overwhelmed their opponents. They gained the massive total of 478 MPs, which included 133 Lloyd George Liberals compared with only 28 Asquithians. Indeed the recently relaunched Labour party took up more seats on the opposition benches than the Liberals, 63 of its candidates being returned. Once again the electoral system distorted the actual proportions of support for the parties among the voters. Thus the coalition obtained only 47.6 per cent of the votes cast but 67.6 per cent of the seats. Nevertheless with Irish Unionist and independent Conservative members they could claim an outright majority of those who polled, which suggests that candidates most clearly identified with the war effort were more popular than those whose records were not unimpeachable on that score. Certainly election literature wherever possible stressed their loyalty to king and country. Curiously only a minority of the forces chose to exercise their vote by post, and those who did apparently were not overwhelmingly disposed to support coalition candidates. It seems that Lloyd George and his supporters gained from the fact that the Representation of the People Act of 1918 had enfranchised all adult males and women over thirty. The new voters, especially women, endorsed his claims that he had won the war and that Germany should be made to pay for it.

Whether Lloyd George deserved the credit for winning the war is highly debatable. After his triumph over Asquith he remained firmly attached to the 'big push' strategy which continued to inflict enormous losses on the western front, particularly at Passchendaele in July 1917, with nothing to show for them. Indeed the Germans came nearer to achieving a breakthrough with their Spring campaign of 1918, when for a few weeks the war actually became one of movement rather than of stagnation. It was the intervention of the United States of America, not the strategic thinking of the war cabinet, which brought Germany to accept the armistice in November 1918. Nevertheless Lloyd George cashed in on it, holding a general election immediately afterwards

25   Stretcher bearers at Passchendaele, 1917

which became known as the 'coupon' election from Asquith's denunciation of the paper which endorsed coalition Liberal candidates and spared them a contest with Conservatives who were also given the 'coupon'.

The 1918 election witnessed a realignment of party forces. Between the wars the Conservatives had a built-in electoral advantage as their rivals were split between a declining Liberal party, which never again commanded a majority in the Commons, and a rising Labour party which, although it formed governments in 1924 and 1929, likewise did not win enough seats to control the lower House until 1945.

After 1918 Lloyd George was dependent upon Conservative support, and when they decided to pull the rug from under his feet in 1922 he fell. His power as prime minister had already waned from its peak at the height of the war. Between 1916 and 1918 he had enjoyed more immediate authority than any premier since Walpole. The electoral truce kept him immune from a general election for the duration of hostilities. He ran a war cabinet of five, supported by an advisory team of unelected and unaccountable experts with temporary accommodation in St James's Park, which became known as the Garden Suburb. His control of the economy through the ministry of munitions and other government agencies set up to direct the war effort was almost totalitarian. All this came to an abrupt end when peace broke out. There had to be a general election. The wartime institutions for directing the economy were wound up. Normal cabinet government returned. Lloyd George basked for a while in the aura of power as he took a major part in the making of the Treaty of Versailles. But thereafter his authority was limited by the political constraints imposed upon him by his Conservative allies.

Among the more serious of these was the restriction of his freedom of manoeuvre with respect to Ireland. He had to accept their special pleading for the six northern counties in the Government of Ireland Act of 1920. Paradoxically they became the only part of Ireland to achieve home rule, since they had previously made it clear that they wished to retain the Union while the Nationalists in the south had sought local autonomy within the United Kingdom. But it proved impossible now to contain the demands for independence which had become irresistible since the Easter rising of 1916. After attempting to coerce their advocates into submission with forces known as 'black and tans', from their mixed military and police uniforms, Lloyd George tried to come to terms with them in a treaty signed in December 1921. This sought to integrate the Republic of Ireland into the British Empire by granting it dominion status. A majority of republicans agreed and the Irish Free State came into being. Although it was immediately plunged into civil war, the British government did not intervene. Thus the United Kingdom of Great Britain and Ireland came to a bloody end, while that of Great Britain and Northern Ireland came into being.

The rise of the Labour party also revealed the limitations of Lloyd George's freedom of action due to his dependence upon the Conservatives. Both the prime minister and Bonar Law, leader of the Conservative party, recognised the threat posed by the advances Labour had made since the war. Although they obtained only 63 seats in the general election of 1918 they had polled 2,385,472 votes. Moreover by-elections went their way, as did municipal elections in 1919, especially in London where Labour candidates took 573 seats having previously held 48. How to deal with the emergence of Labour as a rival for power became the main obsession of the other parties in the years 1918 to 1922. One solution was to counter their appeal to the new mass electorate by offering radical alternatives and thus choking the cat with cream. Another was to rally the interests most threatened by Labour's declaration of class war and become a party of resistance to socialism. Lloyd George tried both approaches. He refurbished his radical credentials from his pre-war days, and outbid Labour with welfare schemes and the launching of a housing programme to try to fulfil the promise to make Britain a 'land fit for heroes'. National insurance was extended to all employees except farm labourers and domestic servants. A Housing Act of 1919 compelled local authorities to build council houses which would be let at rents subsidised by the state. Unfortunately this policy of outbidding Labour was stopped in its tracks by the need for retrenchment.

The coalition's credibility with Labour was anyway tarnished by their mixed record at dealing with industrial unrest. While they could claim some success at heading off confrontation between employers and some groups of workers, notably the railwaymen, they were totally unsuccessful in dealing with disputes between mine owners and miners. Thus they failed to implement the recommendation of the Sankey Commission that the mines be nationalised. And their efforts to avert the strike of 1921 were counter-productive, alienating the workforce in the coalfields.

Meanwhile Lloyd George made overtures to fuse the Conservatives and the coalition Liberals into a new centre party which would resist Labour. But neither welcomed them. The Liberals thought their best chance of staving off the Labour threat was to reunite as the party of the left, while most Conservatives considered they stood the best chance of forming the party of resistance by breaking with the coalition. The imminence of a general election brought the issue to a head. Should the coalition fight it as it had fought in 1918, or should the parties which composed it make separate appeals to the electorate? Austen Chamberlain, who became Conservative leader when Bonar Law resigned on grounds of ill health, urged the former. But under-secretaries and backbenchers preferred the latter. They were above all motivated by a dislike of Lloyd George, whom they accused of corruption and opportunism. At a meeting in the Carlton Club in October 1922 their views prevailed. Lloyd George resigned as prime minister and Chamberlain as Conservative leader, whereupon Bonar Law replaced both.

In the ensuing general election the Conservatives obtained an overall majority, gaining 55.8 per cent of the seats in the Commons despite polling only 38.5 per cent of the votes cast. This was the lowest percentage of the poll of any single-party government until 1974, due mainly to the divisions among its opponents. Labour became the second largest party in the Commons, having polled over 4 million votes. The Liberals remained hopelessly split between the followers of Lloyd George, who now called themselves National Liberals, and the supporters of Asquith. Between them they obtained 116 seats, 26 fewer than Labour, although they polled almost exactly as many votes. Apart from rural areas of Scotland, North Wales and the west country, however, these were not cast in traditional Liberal constituencies. Liberals were picking up protest votes against the coalition, while Labour was consolidating its hold on mining and industrial districts, many of which had previously been Liberal heartlands.

Bonar Law's triumph was shortlived, for his health quickly declined and he had to resign in May 1923. Stanley Baldwin succeeded him as prime minister. His solution to the main problem which faced his government, unemployment, was to impose tariffs on imports which competed with British goods. Since this policy had never been endorsed by the electorate, he insisted on dissolving parliament in 1923 in order to obtain a mandate for it.

If ever there was a single issue election, therefore, that held in 1923 was one. Protection was guaranteed to drive a wedge between Conservatives and Liberals. National and Asquithian Liberals came together in a united party to campaign against it on a platform of free trade. Protection was also intended to be an alternative to Labour's proposals for controlling the economy by nationalisation and raising revenue by a 'capital levy', both of which were denounced as 'Bolshevism' by their rivals.

In fact Labour was the chief beneficiary at the polls, gaining 191 seats, an increase of 49 on its total in 1922. The Liberals took 159, 43 more than at the previous election. Most of these gains were at the expense of the Conservatives, who polled almost exactly the same numbers and percentage of voters, but found their members reduced to 258. Labour intensified its grip on inner city constituencies, including a real advance in Greater London from 16 to 37, giving it a parliamentary base in the capital for the first time. The Liberals took seats from Conservatives in counties and middle-class suburbs. Most of these gains were made by Asquithian Liberals, since the former members of the coalition had been cushioned by having no Conservative opponents, a situation now reversed to the National Liberals' cost. The Liberal performance has been seen as a genuine revival. Certainly they polled almost as many votes as the Labour party, obtaining 29.6 per cent of those cast compared with 30.5 per cent. They could not yet be written off as the third party in the British political system.

Yet at the next election, held in 1924, this was to become their fate. Ironically they brought it upon themselves by their decisions first to support and then to overthrow the first Labour government.

The decision to support a Labour government was taken partly because the alternative, to uphold a minority Conservative government, was unthinkable, and partly because it was confidently expected that when Labour demonstrated its incompetence the Liberals rather than the Conservatives would benefit. The first alternative was not practical politics in 1923 since the clash between protection and free trade had been the main issue at the polls. It was rather like a re-run of the 1906 election, with Labour's proposals regarded as of minor importance. Although the Liberals had denounced 'socialism' they had kept Baldwin in their sights as the main target. They therefore supported a Labour motion of no confidence which brought Baldwin's government down in January 1924. The choice of the second option was a miscalculation, however, as Labour did not prove incompetent in government.

On the contrary, fears that a regime of working men and trade unionists would prove to be revolutionary were quickly allayed. So far from threatening to overthrow the system the government of Ramsay MacDonald was reassuringly conformist. The budget brought in by the chancellor of the exchequer Philip Snowden raised no new taxes and lowered the incidence of old ones. Not only was there no capital levy, there was no nationalisation either. The only radical initiative was a Housing Act sponsored by the minister of health, Wheatley, which increased the provision of council housing. Otherwise the first experience of Labour in power was a disappointment to its more socialist supporters. Yet the complaints from the left of its lack of achievement need to be considered in the context of the time. It was not a ministry which could have forced a left-wing socialist programme through parliament, where it was entirely dependent upon Liberal and even Conservative votes for its day-to-day survival. There were ministers from both parties in the cabinet. Even so it suffered ten defeats in Commons divisions. It was only in office for nine months.

Its downfall came over a relatively trivial incident. An article by J. R. Campbell in the *Workers' Weekly* called upon troops not to shoot strikers. The director of public prosecutions determined that this was an incitement to mutiny and had Campbell arrested. Under pressure from Labour backbenchers the attorney general was persuaded to drop the case. The Conservatives put down a vote of censure against the government for interfering with the judiciary. The Liberals proposed an amendment to it calling for a select committee of inquiry. MacDonald, maintaining that the only verdict on the affair he would accept was that of the electorate, made this a vote of censure. His government was defeated by 364 votes to 199. The following day parliament was dissolved.

Labour and Conservative candidates entered the campaign in 1924 in confident mood. By-elections had gone in favour of the government since the previous contest. The party's machinery was improved and more seats were contested than ever before. The Conservatives had also overhauled their organisation since their defeat in 1923, and had dropped protection as a cause. By contrast the Liberals were in poor shape. They only fielded candidates in 340 constituencies. Poor morale as well as lack of money lay behind the failure to provide enough candidates to win a majority.

The 1924 campaign was dirty. Despite the studied moderation of the Labour government the Conservative press from the outset indulged in a 'red scare', culminating in the *Daily Mail*'s publication of the so-called 'Zinoviev letter' purportedly from the president of the Communist International to the British Communist party urging sedition. These tactics probably did the Labour party no harm, but served as a good excuse for their defeat after the election was over.

For Labour was defeated, their seats dropping from the 191 of 1923 to 151. But this was nothing compared with the annihilation of the Liberals, who obtained a mere 40. The beneficiaries were the Conservatives, who won 419. Again the 'winner takes all' element in the electoral system meant that the numbers of seats distorted the support which voters gave the parties. The Conservatives polled 48.3 per cent of the votes cast, Labour 33 per cent and the Liberals 17.6 per cent. Nevertheless the Liberal defeat was catastrophic. Asquith lost Paisley in a straight fight with Labour by 2,228 votes. Elsewhere thirty-one Liberal MPs came third in three-cornered contests. The most significant outcome of the 1924 election was not the Conservative victory, but the fact that it marks the moment when Labour became the only real rival for power to the victors.

8

From Baldwin to Attlee

The triumph of the Conservatives in 1924 was the victory of a pragmatic conservatism which was to predominate in the party for the next forty years. It was not 'right wing' or 'reactionary' nor even ideological, except in the negative sense of being anti-socialist. Baldwin had pulled off the feat of making it the party of resistance to socialism, squeezing the Liberals almost to extinction in the process. He realised that he had picked up the votes of many who had formerly voted Liberal, and did not want to alienate their support. He was convinced that he owed his majority in the Commons to his party's 'creating an impression throughout the country that we stood for stable government and for peace in the country between all classes of the community'.

Stanley Baldwin epitomised this conservatism based on class reconciliation rather than conflict. So far was he from being the class warrior some historians have made of him that he said of trades unions and employers' federations, 'The only progress that can be obtained in this country is by these two bodies of men…learning to understand each other and not to fight each other.' This conviction was instinctive rather than intellectual, for the prime minister was no deep thinker, but he instinctively felt what the average Conservative voter was thinking. He exploited this insight in the radio broadcasts he made and his appearances in cinema newsreels. His adroit exploitation of the new media made him the first British politician whose voice and face were familiar to the general public. Sucking confidently on his pipe, his pockets bulging with tobacco tins, Baldwin breathed reassurance, common sense and above all 'safety first'. He was not going to rock the boat.

The general strike, the most serious industrial dispute of the century, when Baldwin aligned his government with the employers against organised labour, seems at odds with this image. To see the strike as a battle in the class war, with the government siding with the ruling class against the workers, is however to misread the mood of the 1920s.

At the heart of the matter was the special place of the coal industry both in the economy and in the labour movement. Coal mining still employed a million workers, one-fifth of the unionised labour force in 1926. Before 1914 the industry exported between 20 and 25 per cent of its output. By 1920 it exported only 10.8 per cent. The main cause of this decline was the poor productivity of British pits in comparison with foreign competitors. When the mines were handed back to their former owners in 1921 they determined to improve their competitive position by reducing the wages of miners. The Miners' Federation of Great Britain called a strike against this policy, hoping for the assistance of their allies the National Union of Railwaymen and the National Transport Workers. But the Triple Alliance failed to produce a stoppage on the agreed date of 15 April 1921, which became notorious as 'Black Friday' leaving a legacy of guilt in the labour movement.

In 1925 the Conservative government went back to the gold standard which had been abandoned in 1919 and restored the exchange rate of $4.86 to the pound. This crucial decision was largely dictated by the requirements of the City of London, led by the Bank of England. Its influence was such that any government, Conservative, Labour, Liberal or coalition, would have accepted the governor of the Bank's advice that the time was ripe for adopting the gold standard again. It is true that John Maynard Keynes criticised it, and claimed it over-valued sterling; but he had yet to change the conventional wisdom on such matters. Certainly Labour did not alter the policy when it came to power in 1929, and Britain remained on the gold standard until the effects of the European banking crisis forced it off in 1931. Though the decision delighted the City it dismayed manufacturers who saw it as another blow to their ability to compete in export markets. Many sought to offset its effects by forcing further wage cuts, a policy adopted by the coal-owners in June. The Miners' Federation determined to resist such cuts and appealed to the Trades Union Congress to call for sympathetic strikes to back up their resistance. The government intervened by offering to subsidise miners' wages for nine months to make up the difference between their present levels and the 10 per cent reduction proposed by the owners. Meanwhile a royal commission was appointed to investigate the coal industry. The miners accepted this temporary solution, and the strikes were called off on 31 July, which became known as 'Red Friday', redeeming the dishonour of 15 April 1921.

When the royal commission reported in March 1926, however, it could only recommend immediate reductions in costs, including wages, and propose reorganisation of the industry as a long-term solution. The owners accepted the report, but proposed either to reduce wages or, something which the commission had rejected, increase the hours worked for them. This the miners refused with the slogan 'not a penny off the pay, not a minute on the day'. They wanted reorganisation to take place first, and meanwhile for the subsidy to continue. With the subsidy due to end on 30 April the owners gave notice of their intention to pay reduced wages from 1 May. On that day a special meeting of the TUC was charged with responsibility for negotiating with the government to extend the subsidy in order to buy time for some compromise to be reached. If the government refused then a national stoppage would be called.

The negotiations were held and were still in train, albeit to nobody's real satisfaction, on 3 May when the cabinet abruptly ended them on the grounds that compositors at the *Daily Mail* had refused to set type for an editorial denouncing the threat to strike. The notion that the message from the *Mail*'s editor was collusive can be discounted, though it got the government off the hook of prolonged and inconclusive negotiations. Contingency plans had already been made to sustain essential supplies in the event of a general strike.

So the strike began at a minute to midnight on 3 May. It was not general so much as national, since the TUC did not call upon all unions to stop work immediately. First they called out the 'front line' workers in the building, gas, electricity, printing and transport industries. Others were held in reserve. The response was superb. Over 2 million unionists struck. This solidarity stunned contemporaries and has sustained speculation ever since. To the revolutionary left here was a demonstration of the militancy of the labour movement which could have been directed against the state. It was the supineness and betrayal of the bureaucratic trade union leaders which let them down. But did it? The workers were not being asked to bring down the government. They were not even being asked to demand better conditions from their own bosses. They were simply being asked to show solidarity with the miners. Their willingness to do so was magnificent, and as A. J. P. Taylor says 'deserves more than a passing tribute'. It was a generous gesture of support for the miners, who had such a hold over the affections of the labour movement. Where 'Red Friday' had redeemed the honour, the general strike wiped out the guilt of 'Black Friday'.

Perhaps they did deserve more than the apparently craven leadership of the TUC. Yet once the threat of a national stoppage had failed to get concessions from the government, the reality was scarcely likely to do so. As Neville Chamberlain put it, 'We can't afford to destroy public confidence in ourselves by appearing to run away.' The ministers drew a distinction between the miners' strike, or rather lock-out, which was an industrial dispute, and the general strike which they claimed was a constitutional issue. Churchill took up the theme of 'who rules?' with a vengeance in the official *British Gazette*, which was the ministerial mouthpiece during the strike. The TUC had lost a trick in calling out the print workers, since it proved difficult to mount a campaign to counter government propaganda, especially as the BBC was used by the authorities to condemn the strike. The prime minister broadcast an appeal to the nation in which he vowed that he would 'not surrender the safety and the security of the British constitution'.

Thus the ministers called the TUC's bluff. The General Council wanted to help the miners, not to bring down the government. The labour movement was divided anyway, since the bulk of the parliamentary Labour party was opposed to direct action. As Ramsay MacDonald put it, 'The general strike...is clumsy and ineffectual...if the wonderful unity in the strike...would be shown in politics, Labour could solve the mining and similar difficulties through the ballot box.' An offer by the chairman of the royal commission to bring forward proposals for reorganising the coal industry before wages were reduced got the TUC off the hook, even though it did not bind the government. On 12 May they called off the general strike. It had proved to be the original nine days' wonder.

'I thank God for your decision,' Baldwin told the TUC. In victory he was not vindictive, and nor was Churchill, who took over the negotiations with the coal industry when the prime minister went on holiday. Yet neither was able to produce a settlement satisfactory to the miners, who stayed out until November when starvation forced them back.

Though the cabinet attempted to be conciliatory, the Conservative backbenchers sought revenge. They supported the passing of the Trades Disputes Act in 1927 which carried two measures against the trades unions. One made strikes for a political rather than an industrial objective illegal. The other obliged members of unions to contract in rather than out of the Labour party levy on their subscriptions. These measures, however, were counter-productive. No prosecution was brought under the act before its repeal in 1945. Although Labour party funds were hard hit at first, this does not appear to have been a handicap in the next general election, when they obtained 288 seats, making them the biggest party in the House and enabling them to form their second minority government.

The general election of 1929 was the first to be held under full adult suffrage, women over twenty-one having been enfranchised the year before. Whether this made any difference to the outcome cannot be discerned. At the time it was held to have helped Labour, but in view of by-election trends against the government in the run-up to the election it seems possible that it enabled the Conservatives to do rather better than they might have done. As it was they got the highest share of the votes cast, 38.2 per cent, but only 260 seats. The Liberals polled 23.4 per cent but obtained only 59 seats. It seems that the Liberal challenge, which was serious compared with their dismal showing at the previous election, helped Labour candidates. Many who had voted Conservative in 1924 for want of a Liberal candidate returned to their party allegiance in 1929.

The Liberal revival had been largely engineered by Lloyd George, whose old rival Asquith retired to the Lords in 1926 and died in 1928. For once the party leader spent freely from the controversial fund he had amassed as prime minister through the sale of honours. He also had a superb manifesto, largely the work of the economist Keynes, entitled *We can conquer unemployment*. This proposed state expenditure of some £250,000,000 to employ 600,000 men on the construction of roads and houses. Its break with orthodox treasury finance to stimulate economic activity marked a major change in economic policy, by contrast with the lacklustre manifestos on offer

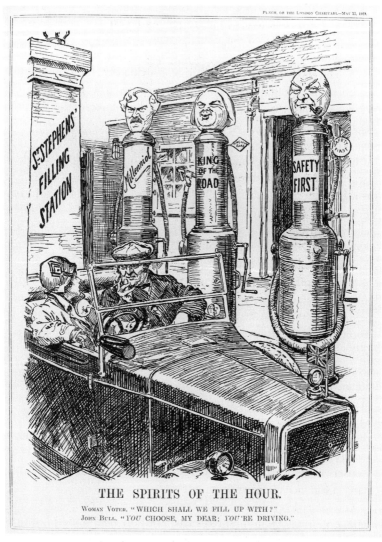

THE SPIRITS OF THE HOUR.

WOMAN VOTER. "WHICH SHALL WE FILL UP WITH?"
JOHN BULL. "*YOU* CHOOSE, MY DEAR; *YOU'RE* DRIVING."

26 'The spirits of the hour', satirising the arrival of full female suffrage

from their rivals. The Conservatives' *Safety First* was held at the time to have been complacent with unemployment running at 1,216,000. As for the Labour manifesto, *Appeal to the Nation*, its main proposal was to increase unemployment benefits.

The second Labour government had scarcely taken office when it was overwhelmed by an economic earthquake that shook the world. Previous post-war governments had been faced with problems caused by the decline of staple industries and the need to repay war debts to the United States of America. Yet these were little local difficulties in comparison with those presented by a glut of primary produce, in what would now be called 'third world' countries, causing prices to plummet and making them unable to pay for the developed world's industrial goods. The result was over-production, a collapse of confidence, stock market crashes, and a sharp rise in unemployment.

Any government would have been severely shaken by the sheer magnitude of the crisis. A minority government dependent upon the votes of other parties for its survival was particularly susceptible to exercising caution rather than courage in tackling it. But the timidity and sheer incompetence of the ministers primarily responsible for coping with the chaos, especially the chancellor of the exchequer Philip Snowden, compounded the difficulties. Oswald Mosley, the chancellor of the Duchy of Lancaster, alone seemed to be pointing a way out of the wilderness when he recommended deficit spending on public works to beat unemployment. Frustrated at the refusal of two cabinet committees to accept his proposals, he resigned, to stay in the political wilderness for the rest of his career.

It has been suggested that MacDonald should have sacked Snowden instead, but that option was simply not on at the time. Labour MPs frustrated with the caution of the prime minister and his chancellor were equally unimpressed by Mosley, whom they regarded as flashy and superficial. Besides, financial orthodoxy required the government to balance its budget rather than to go into the red, spending money on public works. The cost of paying unemployment benefits to over two million on the register by the start of 1931 was already piling up a deficit predicted to reach £120,000,000 by 1932. A committee set up to recommend ways of averting that fate advised cuts of £96,500,000, £67,000,000 of which was to be saved by cutting unemployment benefits. This was unpalatable medicine for a government which claimed to represent the working class. Nevertheless the cabinet economy committee was prepared to recommend pruning the budget by £78,500,000, £43,000,000 of which was to come off unemployment benefits and the rest from the wages of people on the government's payroll such as policemen and teachers. The full cabinet baulked at these savings, and reduced the total to £56,000,000, a figure regarded as too high by the TUC but too low by the parliamentary opposition. Foreign confidence in the adequacy of the measures, and even more in the competence of the ministers, caused a run on the pound, leading the Bank of England to urge tougher measures to prevent devaluation. The cabinet discussed the addition of a further £20,000,000 of cuts to the package, bringing the reduction in unemployment benefit to 10 per cent. The ministers were divided, with eleven supporting the proposal while eight opposed it. MacDonald adjourned the meeting to the following day. When the cabinet reconvened on 24 August he informed his colleagues that he had seen the king, and had agreed to head a national government which would include Conservatives and Liberals. Three of the ministers agreed to serve with him. The rest were dumbfounded. At that moment a gulf opened up between MacDonald and the Labour party which became permanent in September when those members who supported the national government were expelled. The few who continued to support the prime minister became known as National Labour, and were ever after execrated as traitors to the party which they had helped to build up, but to which they also owed their political careers until 1931.

The national government was very much the brainchild of the king. George V persuaded MacDonald to stay on as prime minister and Baldwin and Herbert Samuel, leaders of the Tory and (with Lloyd George providentially incapacitated at the time) Liberal parties to serve under him. Ironically it failed to achieve the object for which it had ostensibly been formed – the maintenance of the parity of the pound. Initial confidence in the new government evaporated when sailors stationed at Invergordon mutinied in protest at the cuts in their pay. The subsequent flight from the pound led to the abandonment of the gold standard on 21 September.

The problem of what to do next to solve the nation's economic problem caused some debate between the protectionists and free traders in the cabinet. This led to the decision to hold a general election to seek a 'doctor's mandate' to do whatever would be deemed necessary to restore the economy to health.

Looked at in terms of gains and losses for the government and the opposition, the general election of 1931 witnessed the biggest landslide in British electoral history. At the end of the polling the national government had won 554 seats, 473 of which were held by Conservatives, the largest number any single party has ever had since 1832. The opposition numbered 61, of whom 52 were Labour. Yet the peculiar circumstances in which the campaign took place, as well as the distorting effects of the electoral system, need to be considered as they somewhat qualify the impression conveyed by a government majority of 493. Only one major party fought the election united: the Conservatives. They had been divided since 1929 on the issue of Empire free trade, a cause espoused by the press barons Beaverbrook and Rothermere, who had even run candidates at by-elections against official Conservatives. At one time the disruption in the party seemed likely to topple Baldwin from the leadership. But the breach was healed after the defeat of an Empire free trade candidate by a Conservative at a by-election in March 1931. By the time of the general election the Conservatives had closed ranks. Meanwhile Labour had split between the rump which supported the national government and the rest who opposed it. The Liberals were even more divided, between Liberal Nationals who saw eye to eye with the Conservatives on the question of protection; adherents of Samuel who, while supporting the government, still advocated free trade; and a handful associated with Lloyd George, now restored to his usual vigour and very much opposed to the government.

Conservatives, National Labour and Liberal Nationals by and large did not field candidates against each other. But of 118 Samuelite Liberals 81 had to stand against Conservative candidates. The divided Liberals were also demoralised, and fielded only 159 candidates, though they claimed they would have contested 300 seats if this had been a normal election. Even that was an admission that they were not in a position to bid for power. This meant that where there had been 447 three-cornered contests in 1929, in 1931 there were only 99. Electors who had voted Liberal two years before switched in droves to the Conservatives, while a minority of them either abstained or voted Labour. All told the various Liberal candidates polled only 10.7 per cent of the votes cast, though curiously they picked up seventy-two seats, twenty more than the Labour party obtained despite its 30.6 per cent of the poll. Labour in fact did not perform quite as disastrously in this election as their meagre fifty-two seats suggests. The party put up 516 candidates, compared with National Labour's paltry 20. These polled 6,649,630 votes. Although this was 1,739,882 less than the total Labour vote in 1929, overall about one million fewer people voted in 1931 than at the previous election, most of them probably Liberal and Labour voters at the first who abstained at the second. Clearly some former Labour voters also polled for the Conservatives in 1931, for their huge total of 11,978,745 votes cannot just have come from their traditional supporters and Liberal defectors. Indeed the government could claim to be truly 'national', in that it rested on middle- and working-class electoral support which had previously upheld Liberal and Labour candidates. The Liberal vote was virtually annihilated, while the Labour vote was pushed into the heartlands of such depressed areas as South Wales. The national government reflected a genuine consensus.

One sign that the vast majority still accepted the dialogue between the major parties as the legitimate context of politics was the derisory showing of the Communists and Oswald Mosley's 'New party' at the polls. The Communist party put up twenty-six candidates and the New party twenty-four. The former polled 74,824 votes and the latter 36,377. The puny performance of the New party was even more disastrous than the figures suggest, for two of their candidates were sitting members who had defected from the Liberal and Labour parties since 1929, yet they polled only 3 and 4 per cent of the votes cast in their respective constituencies.

Since the overwhelming support for the national government came from Conservatives it was not surprising that the 'doctor' prescribed protection for the ailing economy. In 1932 an Imports Act imposed a general tariff on most imports, exceptions being made for raw materials, foodstuffs and imperial produce. The following year the notion of imperial preference was taken further at a conference in Ottawa, but the dominions were not enthusiastic for it and all that ensued were minor agreements. Even so these were sufficient to lead to the departure of the Samuelite Liberals from the government, though they did not go over to the opposition until 1933, leaving behind the

Liberal Nationals who merged with the Conservatives before the general election of 1935. By then the idea that the government was national rather than Conservative was little more than a myth, since Ramsay MacDonald had retired as prime minister and had been replaced by Stanley Baldwin. The myth nevertheless suited Baldwin himself, who had always preferred to lead the Conservatives from left of centre, and knew that the overwhelming majority the party enjoyed in the Commons would have given the right much more of a say in policy if the notion of a coalition could have been set aside.

The 1935 election took place in the context of an international crisis brought about by the Italian invasion of Abyssinia. The League of Nations called upon members to apply economic sanctions to Italy, a call which the national government answered. Collective security thus became an issue in the November election. The government hoped to benefit from its support of the League, since Labour had become identified with pacifism at the East Fulham by-election held in October 1933, when the party had taken the seat from the Conservatives in a campaign which allegedly was won by opposing rearmament. Meanwhile an unofficial referendum known as the 'peace ballot' held in 1934 had shown substantial support for sanctions against an aggressor. Although the government's manifesto put the League of Nations and defence at the top of the list of issues, in fact they became relatively unimportant in the campaign. Labour could point out that it too supported sanctions, for, while its ranks had been divided over rearmament at the party conference that year, the pacifist leader George Lansbury had been ousted after the hawkish speech by Ernest Bevin and had been replaced by Clement Attlee, who made a virtue out of the fact that he had been an officer in the First World War. The party leaders anyway tended to exaggerate the impact of international questions on the electorate. Even the East Fulham by-election turned more on housing and unemployment than on defence, which was true of the general election too.

The by-election victory for Labour was one of several which they won in the run-up to the 1935 polls, which along with municipal gains, including the capture of the London County Council in 1934, gave the party hopes of recovering from the disaster of 1931. They made some recovery, but not enough to regain the ground lost since 1929. In those constituencies which witnessed straight fights between Conservative and Labour candidates at all three elections, the swing from Labour to Conservative had averaged 15.1 per cent between 1929 and 1931, whereas the swing back to Labour was only 9.9 per cent. The Liberals, by contrast, continued to decline. Their share of the vote in constituencies which witnessed three-cornered contests at the three elections went down from 35.8 per cent in 1929, to 29.5 per cent in 1931, to 26.6 per cent in 1935. The result was another electoral endorsement for the national government led by Baldwin. His Conservative colleagues obtained 388 seats, the Liberal Nationals 35 and the National Labour 8, a government total of 431. Since the distinction between the 'parties' making up the national 'coalition' was now mainly academic, some commentators decline to make it and see this as a Conservative total. Labour took 154 seats, Lloyd George and Samuelite Liberals 19, the Independent Labour party, which had split with Labour in 1932 and fought the election separately, 4, and others, including two Communists, 7. Thus the national government had an overall majority of 247.

The paradox of the Conservative party, albeit as part of a national government, winning the only two elections to be held in the thirties, the 'devil's decade' of unemployment has been endlessly debated. Labour's poor showing in particular has been explained variously. At the time, the hostility of the press apart from the *Daily Herald*, and the divisive party conference which produced a new and uncharismatic leader just before the polls, seemed to be paramount. Baldwin also 'came across' better in the more objective media of newsreels and radio broadcasts. The continued decline of the Liberal party has been seen as a factor. The Liberals managed to put up only 159 candidates at this election, and former Liberals apparently switched to the Conservatives rather than Labour after the debacle of 1931. But that Baldwin was genuinely popular with the working class seems to be a principal cause of his government's success. His appeal to those in work, whose standard of living rose during the decade, is now established, and in 1935 unemployment dropped for the fourth year running to just over 2 million. But he also seems to have appealed even to unemployed workers, for the swing against his government was remarkably uniform throughout the country, around 9.4 per cent, and showed no significant variation in areas where the depression was still severe. Perhaps here the linking of rearmament with the reduction of unemployment in the most depressed areas, which Neville Chamberlain made explicitly in an election speech at Glasgow, struck a winning note. The placing of admiralty orders for the construction of nine warships in yards with the heaviest unemployment drove the message home. Whatever the reasons, as in 1931 so in 1935 Baldwin's brand of Conservatism was based on a widespread consensus.

Even broader than the Baldwin consensus was the almost universal adulation of the royal family and the monarchy. This was tested by the abdication of Edward VIII. George V, whose popularity at the time of his silver jubilee in May 1935 had probably benefited the national government in that election year, died the following January. There was more than a generation gap between the old king and his ministers and the incoming monarch; there was a gaping gulf of values. George had upheld Victorian values at his court. Decorum at royal functions was strictly upheld. Dress was formal. No divorced men or women were invited to attend. The forty-year-old Prince of Wales threatened those values. His style in clothes was the subject of a disapproving memorandum drawn up by Neville Chamberlain, though suppressed by the prime minister. More seriously, he wished to marry an American woman who had not only been divorced before, but had to obtain a divorce from her second husband, Mr Simpson, before she could be free to become Edward's wife.

Baldwin managed as it were to divorce the monarch from the monarchy. Edward VIII was dethroned, but the crown retained its hold on the nation. This feat was partly made possible by the maladroitness with which the king's friends mishandled their attempt to generate support for him. There were elements at all levels of society, from Conservative MPs to unemployed workers, who sympathised with his plight. The king himself visited South Wales shortly after his accession and expressed concern at the social conditions he encountered, while the Chamberlain memorandum rebuked him for such public expressions. But his principal supporters, Winston Churchill and the press barons Beaverbrook and Rothermere, got nowhere with their campaign to exploit these sympathies. Edward also let them down, backing off from broadcasting an appeal to the public when Baldwin disapproved of it. As Beaverbrook complained to Churchill, 'Our cock won't fight.'

In fact the forces of reaction were overwhelming. The stance

Baldwin made was applauded by all sections of British, and especially English, society. The prime minister was greeted as enthusiastically as the new king, George VI, at the coronation in May 1937. As one correspondent congratulated him after the formal abdication in December 1936: 'You have kept our Empire united and, by making it plain that the idea of moral dignity is for our people inseparable from that of the throne, you have raised that throne higher than ever in the esteem of the world.'

Another supporter of Baldwin's stance at the time of the crisis hoped that he would be 'long with us to guide the ship of state through the shoals of fascism and communism'. In fact he resigned shortly after the coronation, to be succeeded as prime minister by Neville Chamberlain. Nevertheless the ship of state did avoid these extremes.

The British Union of Fascists, founded by Sir Oswald Mosley after his return from Italy in 1932, never fully recovered from the violence of his blackshirts at the Olympia rally in 1934. 'Respectable' elements among his backers withdrew their support, and the BUF became more and more associated with anti-semitic demonstrations in London's East End, Leeds and other cities with large Jewish populations. Its failure to fight the 1935 election was a sign of its meagre support. Its violence led to the passing of the Public Order Act in 1936 to ban political uniforms and to restrict provocative marches.

If the government showed that it was prepared to stand up to fascists at home, however, its stance against those abroad was less impressive. Mussolini got away with his annexation of Abyssinia without much beyond verbal resistance from Britain. Hitler occupied the Rhineland in 1936 with no difficulty. And when the Spanish Civil War broke out the British government announced a policy of non-intervention, even though this played into the hands of the fascists there who received help from Germany, Italy and Dr Salazar, the right-wing dictator of Portugal. Yet these alarming developments changed public attitudes towards rearmament. Where up to 1935 the government was criticised for spending too much on defence, after 1937 it was opposed for not spending enough. Even the Labour party stopped opposing the defence estimates in that year, while the shadow foreign secretary boldly stated that 'our country must be powerfully armed'. More forthright criticism was forthcoming from the Conservative benches articulated most vociferously by Churchill. He had pressed Baldwin to increase the size of the air force to meet the German challenge, and though at first he did not oppose Chamberlain's defence policy he became its most bitter critic after the resignation of the foreign secretary Anthony Eden in 1938. Churchill's condemnation of the 'appeasement' of Nazi Germany's designs on Czechoslovakia, particularly Chamberlain's flight to Munich in 1938, earned him a rebuke from his constituency party, until the invasion of Prague in 1939 vindicated him and silenced his critics.

The annexation of Czechoslovakia changed the government's policy towards Germany overnight. A guarantee was given to Poland that any violation of her territorial integrity would provoke a response from Britain and France. When the Germans invaded Poland late in August, an ultimatum was issued that if they did not withdraw Britain would declare war. On the expiry of the allotted time on 3 September 1939 Chamberlain broadcast to the nation that it was at war with Germany. There was none of the wild excitement of 1914; more a universal resignation that Hitler must be resisted.

Anticipating German disregard of the ultimatum Chamberlain formed a war cabinet to which he appointed Winston Churchill as first lord of the admiralty. Churchill had waited a long time for this vindication of his stance on the question of preparedness for war. He had spent much of the thirties writing a biography of his great ancestor the Duke of Marlborough. As the four volumes unfolded, he identified himself more and more with Marlborough and his times. Thus he wrote of 'the conquering hero' of the battle of Blenheim: 'The pursuit of power with the capacity and in the desire to exercise it worthily is among the noblest of human occupations. But Power is a goddess who admits no rival in her loves.' He introduced the final volume pointing out that 'it exposes and explains the lamentable desertion by England of her leadership of the Grand Alliance, or League of Nations, which had triumphantly broken the military power of Louis XIV. It shows how when Victory has been won across measureless hazards it can be cast away by the pride of a victorious War Party and the intrigues of a pacifist reaction.' Now he was in a position to right the wrongs of both.

Had a general election been held in 1939 or 1940 the signs are that the Conservatives would have won again. As late as January 1940 a Gallup poll still showed that a majority preferred Chamberlain as prime minister. When in April public opinion was polled on the question of

Chamberlain's successor, 28 per cent chose Anthony Eden and 25 per cent Churchill; only 6 per cent opted for Attlee. Yet the following month Chamberlain was forced to step down after a parliamentary debate which criticised his government's handling of an expedition to Norway, and Winston Churchill formed a coalition government. His war cabinet of five included the Labour leader as deputy prime minister.

Labour politicians in fact played a major role in the wartime coalition. Ernest Bevin, who had been general secretary of the Transport and General Workers' Union from 1919 to 1940, became minister of labour. Herbert Morrison was made minister of supply in 1940 and then became home secretary. Hugh Dalton was minister of economic warfare from 1940 to 1942 and president of the board of trade from 1942 to 1945. Their records as ministers largely responsible for domestic concerns buried the notion that Labour was 'unfit to govern', which their opponents had hurled at their predecessors, and which the performance of the second Labour government had seemed to justify.

Public opinion also moved to the left during the war. The widespread acceptance of the Beveridge report after its publication in 1942 showed that a return to high unemployment would be politically unacceptable when peace returned. It also recommended a free health service and family allowances. Labour and Liberal MPs were noticeably more enthusiastic about implementing its recommendations than were the Conservatives. A Conservative minister of education, however, R. A. Butler, was largely responsible for the Education Act of 1944, which committed post-war governments to universal free education to the age of fifteen. Nevertheless Labour benefited from plans for post-war reconstruction, as its massive and increasing lead in Gallup polls in the run-up to the 1945 general election indicated.

Insofar as the polls indicated not so much support for Labour as antipathy towards the Conservatives, this was almost certainly due, not to that party's record on pre-war economic problems, but to its being identified with appeasement and the perceived failure to prepare the nation for war. A hard-hitting pamphlet, *Guilty Men*, which went through several editions during the war, painted a grim picture of the British Expeditionary Force's predicament at Dunkirk in 1940, and sought to lay the blame for it at the feet of the Conservative ministers

27   Campaign posters, 1945, focusing on the leadership of Churchill and on the ills of the inter-war years

of the 1930s. The retreat to the Channel port and the improvised flotilla of boats that got the men back to England might feature in legend as the 'Dunkirk spirit' but the reality was a dreadful defeat for British arms which led to the search for scapegoats. They were found in the persons of Baldwin, Chamberlain and the other alleged appeasers of the thirties. The impact of such propaganda helps to explain why a party led by Churchill, the man who won the war as far as most of his countrymen were concerned, lost the election. For although Conservatives tried to cash in on his reputation – the party manifesto was titled *Mr Churchill's Declaration of Policy to the Electors* – he had been the chief critic of appeasement at the time.

The men who fought in North Africa, Italy and after the 'D-Day' landings of July 1944 in France, the Low Countries and Germany were apparently much influenced by such propaganda. The 'services' vote' which held up the announcement of the election results was estimated to have been more skewed to Labour than the electorate in general. But there is a myth that this swung the election to Labour. In fact there was a widespread swing which gave the Labour party 393 seats to the Conservatives' 213, the Liberals' 12 and others 22, an overall majority of 146. Even then Labour did not poll an overall majority of voters, obtaining 47.8 per cent of votes cast compared with 39.8 per cent for the Conservatives.

This division in the electorate qualifies the notion that there was a consensus behind Labour's policies at the time. To some historians Labour benefited from the general acceptance of state control of industry during the war, and the commitment to social reform after it which all three major parties espoused, but which the electorate thought that the Labour party was most enthusiastic about. To contemporaries, however, the gulf between the parties seemed wide. During the election campaign Churchill, who led a 'caretaker' government when the coalition ended following peace in Europe, inadvisedly predicted that were Labour to win a 'gestapo' would be established in Britain, which was hardly the language of moderation. Another Conservative later said that during the years of Labour rule he felt that he was in an occupied country. Even though something like 2 million middle-class voters must have voted Labour, while eight cabinet ministers, including Attlee himself, had been to public school, the prevailing impression was that the working class, and above all the

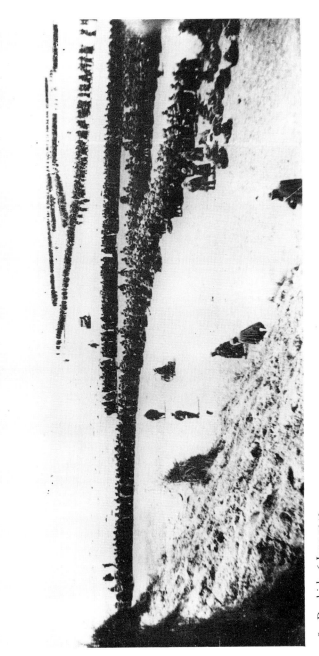

28 Dunkirk, 6 June 1940

trade union movement, represented in the cabinet by the formidable figures of Ernest Bevin, Herbert Morrison and Aneurin Bevan, had taken over the government of the country. 'Thank God for the civil service,' the king is alleged to have said on hearing of the outcome of the election.

The fact was that Bevan had a tremendous struggle with the British Medical Association to get them to accept the National Health Service, during which he had to concede points to them such as the provision of private beds in public wards. Although the nationalisation of coal, gas, electricity, the railways, the Bank of England and Cable and Wireless went through parliament with little resistance, there was a fight over road transport, iron and steel and the sugar refining industry. Labour itself was divided on the merits of extending the system of national-isation to manufacturing as well as services, while the Conservatives found a cause to rally electoral support. The House of Lords' resistance to the nationalisation of iron and steel led the government to amend the 1911 Parliament Act, reducing the time the Upper House could delay bills passed by the Commons from two years to one. The sugar refiners Tate and Lyle fought the proposed nationalisation of their business with a highly effective advertising campaign featuring a cartoon sugar cube called 'Mr Cube'.

The post-war consensus really emerged when the Conservatives realised that unless they improved their electoral appeal they were doomed to remain in opposition indefinitely. Most unusually in modern times the government did not lose a by-election between 1945 and 1950. Moreover Labour gains in municipal elections were enormous, 1,000 seats falling to the party in November 1945 alone. The Conservative party responded to these setbacks by overhauling their electoral machinery. By 1950 their constituency organisations were in better shape than before, while they had 3 million party members, the most ever. They also modified their image by accepting the welfare state and the nationalisation of service, though not of manufacturing, industry. Their commitment to both led them to be labelled semi-socialist when the reaction to the consensus set in at the end of the 1970s. In fact it owed more to the dominance of Liberal ideas expounded by Beveridge and Keynes. In that sense a declining Liberal party, epitomised by Beveridge failing to get into parliament in 1945, left a legacy of social reform and economic management accepted by both Labour and Conservative parties alike. In that ironic sense they could both have said 'We are all Liberals nowadays.'

Even with these measures the Conservatives did not find it easy to replace Labour in office. The government retained a degree of support which is astonishing in view of the economic difficulties which the country faced during the post-war period. Prior to the war, Britain had been a major creditor country, being owed some £3,500,000,000. By 1945 she was a major debtor, owing £2,500,000,000, most of it to the United States. When the Americans ended lease–lend agreements within a month of the conclusion of the war with Japan, it strained Britain's financial system to the limit. Keynes was despatched to Washington to negotiate a loan to bail her out. The USA attached stringent conditions to it, including an agreement to make sterling convertible into dollars. As early as 1947 this aggravated a financial crisis partly brought on by the severest winter of the century. By 1949 the British could not sustain sterling at the level of $4.03 to the pound and devalued it to $2.80 to the pound.

Despite these, and other economic difficulties inherited from the war, Labour won the general election of 1950. The election witnessed a turn-out of 84 per cent, the highest since the advent of adult suffrage. Labour gained from the abolition of plural voting in 1948, whereby graduates had been able to vote for candidates in twelve universities in addition to those in their own constituencies, and businessmen with premises in a constituency other than their domicile could vote in both. But Labour also lost from the redistribution of seats since 1945, whereby nineteen had, for instance, gone from the area of the London County Council. Nevertheless they polled three-quarters of a million more votes than the Conservatives, though their overall majority was reduced to five.

With such a slender majority the Attlee government could ill afford the luxury of ministerial argument. Unfortunately the outbreak of the Korean War, and Britain's military involvement in it – itself a contentious issue in Labour circles – brought about a financial crisis, as defence costs soared, requiring cuts elsewhere in the budget. A prime candidate for savings was the health service, whose estimates rocketed from £228,000,000 in 1949–50 to a projected £387,000,000 in 1951–2. Sir Stafford Cripps as chancellor sought to hold the estimate to £329,000,000 by introducing charges on spectacles and dental treatment. Aneurin Bevan, who rightly regarded the NHS as his own creation, objected violently to this proposal and persuaded Cripps to suspend it. When Hugh Gaitskell succeeded Cripps, however, he reintroduced the principle of charges and provoked Bevan's resignation along with that of Harold Wilson in April 1951.

During the summer the government was overwhelmed by other difficulties. Abroad the nationalisation of the Anglo-Iranian Oil Company complicated foreign relations and exacerbated economic problems. At home a balance of payments deficit grew alarmingly. The chancellor, Gaitskell, flew to the United States to seek American assistance, and was actually in Washington when Attlee unexpectedly got the king to dissolve parliament.

It was an odd decision on the prime minister's part. Gallup polls in October showed a Conservative lead of 50.5 per cent to Labour's 43.5 per cent. Yet in the event the Labour party secured nearly 14 million votes, the highest poll ever achieved by a British political party. The Conservatives ran them a close second with over 13,700,000. Unfortunately for the government their huge total was largely due to massive majorities piling up in safe seats, while their opponents' vote was more evenly distributed, giving them an overall majority of seventeen. It seems that many voters in marginal constituencies who had previously voted Liberal supported the Conservatives. The Liberal vote declined from over 2,600,000 to 730,000 between 1950 and 1951. Largely this was due to the reduction in the number of candidates from 475 to 109. Churchill deliberately cultivated the Liberal vote and offered the leader Clement Davies, one of the six successful candidates, a ministerial post after the election. Davies refused when the new prime minister declined to support proportional representation as a condition of his acceptance. One can understand why the Liberals made it, and why Churchill showed no interest in it, given that neither would have been involved in forming a ministry if there had been a direct correlation between the number of Labour votes and seats.

Not that Labour lost this election just because of the vagaries of the electoral system and the collapse of the Liberal vote. It also saw the return to the Conservative fold of many middle-class suburban voters who had been inclined to support Labour candidates since the war. The Labour slogan 'Fair shares' had hit the right note, keeping alive the wartime spirit of co-operation, through the late forties. Increas-

29   Conservative campaign poster, 1951, depicting Attlee as a
moderate façade for Bevanite socialism

ingly, however, it came to jar. The maintenance of controls, especially
rationing, was irksome, making the Conservative manifesto *Set the
people free* attractive. The failure of Labour's housing programme to
realise more than 200,000 new houses a year, most of them council
houses to rent, also made the Conservative pledge to build 300,000
houses a year, mostly for sale, appealing to the middle classes now
desperately requiring homes for the growing families produced by the

post-war 'baby boom'. At the same time there is evidence that they benefited more than the working class from the welfare state. The commitment of the Conservatives to its preservation, therefore, was a vital ingredient in bringing them back to power. They were to exercise it for thirteen years.

9

From the accession of Queen Elizabeth to the entry into the European Economic Community

One of the reasons why Attlee dissolved parliament unexpectedly in 1951 was to get an election out of the way before King George VI set off on a tour of Australia and New Zealand in January 1952. Ironically for the outgoing Labour government the king had to undergo an operation for lung cancer before the dissolution, which made him unfit for the journey, though he recovered enough for his daughter Princess Elizabeth and her husband the Duke of Edinburgh to fly out to East Africa early in the new year. While they were in Kenya, however, news reached them that he had died and that she was now Queen Elizabeth II.

Much was made at the time of the dawn of a new Elizabethan age. Certainly the general public enthused about the young queen, the coronation, the first to be televised, being watched by millions in June 1953. The only sour note was struck by Scottish nationalists, who objected to her title on the grounds that there had not been a previous Elizabeth on the throne of Scotland. Some even blew up post office letter boxes featuring the initials EIIR. Such 'outrages' alienated most Scots, however, and throughout the fifties the Scottish National party polled very few votes in general elections or by-elections.

Indeed third parties of any kind fared badly at the polls during the period of Conservative hegemony which followed their victory in 1951. It seemed that a two-party system had entrenched itself in British political life, with the Conservatives as the natural ruling party and Labour as its only real opponent.

The Conservatives benefited from the economic growth which

30   The royal family at Balmoral, 1957

marked the opening of the new reign, especially after the end of the
Korean War in 1953. They were able to sustain high levels of
employment, low rates of interest and generally rising standards of
living. They also fulfilled election pledges. Rationing was ended in
1954. The target of 300,000 houses a year was also achieved in 1954 by
the minister of housing and local government, Harold Macmillan.
Road haulage and the steel industry were denationalised. But the
Conservatives retained the other nationalised concerns and upheld the
welfare state. Labour warnings at the general election that a Conservative victory would undo the achievements of the post-war
administration, and bring back the high unemployment of the thirties,
were thus proved to be unfounded.

The continuity from Attlee's last years of office to those of Sir
Winston Churchill was picked up by the press. *The Economist* invented
a cross-party character 'Butskell', a composite of the names of the
Conservative and Labour chancellors of the exchequer R. A. Butler
and Hugh Gaitskell. Other papers adopted the conceit, and coined the
term 'Butskellism' to epitomise the application of Keynesian eco-

nomics to the management of the economy, which successive governments adopted from the 1940s to the 1970s.

But budgets could be used for electoral as well as economic objectives. Butler's budget of 1955 reduced income tax by sixpence in the pound. This was done quite deliberately to influence the outcome of the imminent general election. Churchill, the prime minister, even advocated a reduction of a shilling to boost the government's standing.

Sir Winston had enjoyed the 'Indian summer' of the premiership after his defeat in 1945. But a stroke in 1953 had undoubtedly debilitated him, and by March 1954 his secretary Jane Portal admitted that he was 'getting senile and failing more and more each day'. Nevertheless he stubbornly retained the premiership, to the frustration of his cabinet colleagues. In 1955, however, when he attained the age of eighty-one, even Churchill accepted that it was time to go before the next election. He stepped down as prime minister, being replaced by the man who for long had been regarded as the heir apparent, Sir Anthony Eden. Eden immediately asked the king for a dissolution of parliament.

The general election of 1955 was a triumph for the Conservatives, who increased their majority to fifty-four. This was the first time that a government had actually improved its position at an election since the nineteenth century. It was a remarkably low-key contest. Television made little impact. The BBC transmitted only party political broadcasts, while the newly created independent companies were forbidden to carry political advertisements by the act of parliament which set them up in 1954. This was therefore the last election at which the main influence on public opinion was the newspaper press, which was biased in favour of the Conservatives. Papers such as the *Daily Express* attacked Labour by exploiting the divisions in the party's ranks which had been perpetuated since Bevan resigned from the government in 1951. The Bevanite section of the party was depicted as a sinister extreme socialist faction which really controlled Labour policy, even though Bevan himself had had the whip withdrawn just before the election was called. This adverse image possibly helped the Conservative party to retain a steady 4 per cent lead over Labour in the Gallup polls.

In the event there was a remarkably uniform swing to the Conservatives of 1.8 per cent. The turn-out was down compared with

1951, from 82.5 per cent to 76.8. The Labour vote fell by over a million and a half, while the Conservatives lost only 400,000. This gave the latter 49.7 per cent of the votes cast, the nearest any party has come to obtaining over half since the Second World War. Votes cast for the Liberals, their share of the total, and the number of seats contested – 109 – and which they held – 6 – stayed remarkably constant.

Conservative election propaganda stressed the party's commitment to peace. Their manifesto was titled *United for Peace and Progress* while posters portraying the new prime minister carried the caption chosen by Eden himself, 'working for peace'. Unfortunately for Sir Anthony his long and distinguished career as a diplomatist was to end after he involved Britain in an ill-fated military intervention in Egypt.

Britain had maintained an interest in Egyptian affairs ever since the construction of the Suez Canal and had actually had a base there since the 1880s. In the early 1950s there were at least 70,000 British troops in the Canal Zone, despite the fact that a treaty negotiated with the Egyptians in 1936 restricted the number to 10,000. In 1954 agreement was reached that these would be withdrawn, but Egypt would maintain the base so that the British could reoccupy it in the event of a war in the region. Some Conservative MPs, who became known as the Suez group, protested at this withdrawal.

Soon after the agreement was signed in 1954 Colonel Nasser came to power in Egypt. He was determined to build a dam to control the flow of the Nile, and approached western powers to raise the finance required for its construction. At first Britain, France and the United States of America showed interest, but the Americans backed off in 1956 when Nasser also approached the Soviet Union, and persuaded the other western powers to do likewise. The Egyptian leader then announced that to raise the sums required he would nationalise the Suez Canal. This dictatorial act persuaded the British prime minister that Nasser must be stopped from requisitioning the assets of the Suez Canal Company. Eden, who had earned a reputation in the thirties as being opposed to appeasement, detected parallels between fascist ambitions in Europe and Nasser's objective to lead the Arab world, backed by the Soviet Union. It seemed to him that Khruschev, the Soviet leader, was playing Hitler to Nasser's Mussolini.

Major users of the canal became concerned at the deteriorating relations between Britain, France and Egypt, and sought to resolve the problem peacefully. When Egypt ignored their demands to be consulted, they referred his seizure of the canal to the United Nations, only to have the Soviet Union veto a proposal favouring the Anglo-French view in the security council. This confirmed the conviction of the British and French governments that they might seek to enforce their claims. The United States government made it very clear that they would oppose any use of force.

Nevertheless, British and French ministers determined to use the military option and colluded with Israel to launch an attack upon Egypt which would give them a pretext to intervene to protect the canal. On 29 October Israeli forces invaded Egypt. The following day the British and French issued an ultimatum ordering the belligerents to withdraw to positions ten miles either side of the Suez Canal, while Anglo-French forces occupied the Canal Zone. Since the fighting was occurring to the east of the canal the Israelis concurred but the Egyptians naturally refused. When the ultimatum ran out, British and French planes bombed Egyptian airfields on 31 October. On 5 November troops were parachuted into Port Said. The following day, however, the Egyptians and Israelis agreed to a cease-fire, removing the excuse for Anglo-French armed intervention. That night Britain agreed to call off the military operation.

International reaction was primarily responsible for the British decision. Both the United States and the Soviet Union, in a rare display of unity, called for a cease-fire in the security council of the United Nations, a proposal which Britain blocked by using her veto for the first time. The superpowers then put pressure on the British in very different ways. The USSR threatened to launch a nuclear attack. This was dismissed as bluster and as a device to draw attention from the Soviet suppression of an uprising in Hungary. American measures, however, were taken far more seriously. A run on the pound alarmed the chancellor of the exchequer, Harold Macmillan, converting him from being one of the most hawkish members of the cabinet into a dove. When the United States offered a loan if British forces were withdrawn, he advised acceptance of it. A separate Canadian proposal in the general assembly of the United Nations, calling for the despatch of an international force to separate the belligerents, gave the British government an opportunity to climb down without complete loss of face.

31   Demonstration of Edinburgh University students during the
Suez crisis, November 1956

The national reaction to the Suez crisis threatened to dissolve the
consensus which had bolstered the Conservatives in the general election
of 1955. At first the politicians of both parties denounced the
nationalisation of the Suez Canal, and agreed that Nasser should be
obliged to abandon it. Indeed it was Hugh Gaitskell, who had replaced
Attlee as leader of the opposition, who first compared the Egyptian
leader to Hitler and Mussolini in a Commons debate on the seizure of
the canal. But over the summer the bipartisan agreement was strained
as the government made clear its determination to use force if all else
failed. The Labour party insisted more and more that the problem
should be remitted to the United Nations, while the Suez group of
Conservatives clamoured for an immediate strike against Egypt. The
issuing of the ultimatum was bitterly opposed by Labour in an angry
debate in the House of Commons. Most Conservative MPs sided with
the government, though two ministers resigned in protest. The decision
to abandon the expedition, however, angered and dismayed some
Tories, including the Suez group.

The crisis also divided people outside the House. Demonstrations were organised in Trafalgar Square and other city centres to protest against the use of force. Petitions and telegrams were sent in shoals to Downing Street. By no means all of the messages sent to the prime minister were critical of his actions, however. Society was split from top to bottom by the Suez affair. A Gallup poll taken on 1–2 November showed that 46 per cent disagreed with his handling of the situation in the Middle East, 40 per cent agreed with it, while 14 per cent did not know. The question 'Do you think we were right or wrong to take military action against Egypt?' found 44 per cent answering 'Wrong', 37 per cent answering 'Right', while 19 per cent could express no opinion. This distribution was not just along party lines, for of those who answered 'Right' 68 per cent were Conservative, 24 per cent were Liberal and 16 per cent were Labour supporters. Nor was the split along class lines. The middle classes were divided, with many university students signing petitions for and against the action. As for the working class, many if not most approved the decision to attack Egypt, especially if they had served in the forces there themselves.

The country was thus divided very evenly at the height of the crisis, with a small if significant majority disapproving of the resort to force. Any notion that the government was faced by an overwhelmingly hostile public opinion must be dismissed, especially when after the crisis had passed there was a rallying towards its stance. When Gallup repeated the question, inviting approval or disapproval of the military action in mid-November and early December, 53 per cent of those polled approved while only 32 per cent disapproved. By then the decision to halt the invasion of Egypt could be blamed on the Americans and on the Labour party.

Despite these signs of support for his actions the prime minister was shattered by the Suez crisis. His health had not been good since a botched operation for gallstones in 1953. Now it collapsed, and he was advised to convalesce in the West Indies. On his return he could not face the strain of office and resigned in January 1957. After 'soundings' among leading Conservatives the queen chose Harold Macmillan as his successor.

The Suez fiasco marked the end of more than Eden's political career. It also revealed that Britain was finished as a major power. At the height of the British Empire she had maintained the status of a great power, with spheres of influence around the globe. Canada and islands in the West Indies, swathes of African territory from Kenya to Nigeria and from the Cape of Good Hope to Egypt, the Middle East from Palestine to the Persian Gulf, the East from India to Hong Kong, and the whole of Australasia, had all been shaded in red or pink on maps hung in schoolrooms from Land's End to John o'Groats. But the burden of sustaining these imperial commitments became harder as Britain's economic decline set in. The fall of Singapore in 1942 was a devastating blow to her imperial pretensions. After the Second World War the British retreat from empire was rapid. The independence of India and Pakistan was recognised in 1947 followed a year later by Burma and Ceylon (Sri Lanka). Suez accelerated the process. Ghana and the Malay states became independent in 1957, Cyprus and Nigeria in 1960. Between 1961 and 1964 many former colonies in Africa and the West Indies were recognised as independent states.

One of the burdens of sustaining the status of a major power was defence. Britain did not fully demobilise in 1945 but retained conscription for men over eighteen. In 1950 the armed forces numbered 719,600, most of them conscripts, whose term of national service was extended from eighteen months to two years at the height of the Korean War. While their main task was imperial defence these troops were also stationed in Germany, where Britain maintained a zone in the West and a sector in Berlin. These commitments were reinforced by membership of the North Atlantic Treaty Organisation after 1949. After Suez the Macmillan government took the decision to phase out national service. By 1960 the services had been reduced to 525,600 men, while a decade later they consisted of a completely professional body of 373,000.

While reducing the reliance on conventional forces, the government became more committed to nuclear weapons. Britain's first hydrogen bomb was exploded in the Pacific in May 1957. Critics of this policy launched the Campaign for Nuclear Disarmament early in 1958. Although it was not a party political organisation, many of its leaders were prominent in the Labour movement while most of its supporters probably voted Labour. At all events it became associated with the Labour party's left wing, even though at the party conference held in Brighton in 1957 a motion for unilateral nuclear disarmament had been overwhelmingly defeated, partly as a result of an impassioned plea to reject it made by Bevan.

Indeed, in the run-up to a general election, Bevan and his former opponent Gaitskell displayed a degree of unity unusual for Labour politicians in the 1950s. Certainly disarray in Labour ranks, which undoubtedly affected the party's performance in the 1955 election, cannot be held responsible for their defeat in 1959. And yet defeated they were, giving the Conservatives the unprecedented achievement of improving their position at four consecutive general elections and their majority at three, for they emerged with an overall lead of 265. The Labour vote was slightly down on 1955 and the party's share of the total cast significantly down to 43.8 per cent. This could be largely attributed to the revival in the Liberal fortunes at least at the polls. They polled over twice as many votes as in the previous election, and more than doubled their share of those cast from 2.7 to 5.9 per cent, though the number of Liberal seats in the Commons remained obstinately the same at six. It could be that the Liberals picked up former Conservative supporters who lost their nerve over Suez, for their revival began with by-election victories in 1958, one of them in a safe Conservative seat, the first time since 1929 that the Liberal party had made gains in by-elections. Otherwise there is little sign that the Conservatives were harmed by their association with the crisis. As we have seen they quickly recovered their lead over Labour at the end of 1956, and by 1959 other issues had become more significant. Probably the most crucial element in the election was the rise in the standard of living. The years 1955 to 1960 saw the lowest rate of inflation since the 1930s, and also witnessed a favourable balance of trade. These economic conditions sustained a consumer boom which the Conservatives stressed in their electoral propaganda. Macmillan was alleged to have told a factory worker 'You've never had it so good,' while a poster carried the message 'Life's better under the Conservatives – don't let Labour ruin it.'

Gaitskell determined to change the Labour party's image to one which would appeal to the new electorate. He and other socialist intellectuals argued that the class structure had changed since the early twentieth century. Where three-quarters of the employed population had been manual labourers then, by the late fifties it had gone down to about 60 per cent. At the same time the percentage of white-collar workers had increased from 19 to 36. It had been appropriate to launch a party based on the votes of the newly enfranchised manual workers

" I thought your shirt was off-white — until I saw yours ! "

32   Election cartoons by Cummings of Harold Macmillan and
Hugh Gaitskell, 1959

33   'Joining the club' by Vicky. Cartoon on Macmillan's
abortive attempt to enter the EEC in 1963

in 1918. But that electoral base had been eroded by the 1950s, and unless the party could appeal to managerial and professional people it was doomed to go on losing elections.

Gaitskell concluded from this diagnosis that nationalisation and nuclear disarmament were electoral liabilities which did not appeal to the sector of the electorate it was necessary to attract in order to win elections. He therefore sought in 1959 to persuade the party to drop the clause in its constitution which committed it to nationalisation. This campaign was counter-productive, since it led the left to dig in its heels in defence of the clause, and decreased rather than increased Labour's electoral appeal. When the party conference passed a resolution in favour of unilateral nuclear disarmament in 1960, Gaitskell pledged himself to fight to repeal it, and conducted a campaign which led to the reversal of the commitment in 1961.

In fact Labour's best case against the Conservatives was not one with much electoral appeal at the time. This was that, although Britain's economy was growing absolutely, in relative terms it was in decline, since other industrial nations were experiencing more significant rates of growth. Without some measures to make British manufacturing industry more competitive the gap would widen. As Gaitskell prophesied on television in 1961, 'People will say: oh, the British, of course they're nice people...But when it comes to producing and selling, well somehow or other they haven't got it in them.' He predicted that this would come to pass in ten or twenty years. In fact the first cloud, no bigger than a man's hand, passed over the economic landscape that very year, when the balance of payments slipped ominously into the red. The chancellor of the exchequer sought to arrest the slippage with a pay pause aimed at lowering production costs.

With Labour still in disarray it was the Liberals who benefited from the subsequent reaction against the government. In May 1962 they won a sensational by-election at Orpington, previously regarded as a safe Conservative seat. Labour's vote there at the general election was halved. Macmillan tried to revamp his government's image by dismissing one-third of his cabinet. This, however, merely damaged his reputation for 'unflappability'. The prime minister's ratings in the public opinion polls plummeted. Between 1959 and 1961 he was consistently ahead of Gaitskell in the responses of those asked who was the better leader. From 1961 until the autumn of 1962 the two were neck and neck. But towards the end of 1962 Gaitskell edged ahead. This helped Labour to win two of five by-elections held that November. Unfortunately that winter the Labour leader developed a rare disease, and died suddenly and unexpectedly in January 1963.

By then, however, Macmillan's days in office were numbered. The French, partly in retaliation against his insistence on maintaining Britain's 'special relationship' with the USA, vetoed an application to join the European Economic Community. From then on his government was really adrift, without the prospect of an achievement to offer the electorate at an election which it was generally expected would be held that year. The Nassau agreement, whereby the United States undertook to supply Britain with Polaris missiles, was no substitute for entry into the Common Market which its negotiation had helped to veto. Yet no other major policy objective was in the pipeline. It was this aimlessness which left the Macmillan administration peculiarly vulnerable to what could otherwise have been dismissed, as a previous ministerial crisis had been before the last election, as a 'little local difficulty'.

The Profumo affair burst on the world in June 1963. That the war secretary should be sharing the services of a prostitute with a naval attaché at the Soviet Embassy raised eyebrows and caused mutterings about threats to national security, but did not in itself rock the government. That he lied about it both to the prime minister and the House of Commons did. When Profumo admitted that he had deceived the House, Macmillan's handling of the affair called in question his competence. As with Eden in 1956 a crisis was the occasion rather than the cause of his resigning, for with both ill health would have led them to leave office before long. In Macmillan's case, though, it would surely have been after rather than before the pending election. What is more, many, reflecting on the narrow Labour victory which did occur when an appeal was made to the country, concluded that had he led it himself his party could have won. Such even in his sad decline was the reputation of a politician immortalised by a newspaper cartoonist as 'Supermac'.

In fact the general election was delayed until the last possible moment, making this the longest-lived parliament since the Second World War. When it eventually came both parties fought under different leaders from those who had led them at the previous election. On Gaitskell's death the parliamentary Labour party balloted for his successor, and unexpectedly Harold Wilson, regarded as a left winger since his resignation along with Bevan in 1951, won over the right-wing candidate George Brown. After Macmillan's resignation the usual soundings were taken among leading Conservatives and equally unexpectedly Sir Alec Douglas-Home emerged rather than the heir apparent, R. A. Butler. This seemed to be a gift to Labour, whose chosen ground was 'modernisation'. Sir Alec seemed to epitomise the old-fashioned way of running the country. He had been the fourteenth Earl of Home until an act of parliament passed in 1963 enabled peers to renounce their peerages. He was also apparently 'yesterday's man', having been in politics since the thirties when he had accompanied Chamberlain to Munich. He exuded a 'grouse-moor image', even admitting his ignorance of economics. And yet under him the Conservatives clawed back from the pit of public opinion polls into which they had slid since the Profumo affair, to give Labour a good run for their money.

Harold Wilson dropped much of the rhetoric used by previous Labour leaders, and presented the prospect of a new technological revolution coming to rescue Britain's ailing economy. This seemed to strike the right note as Labour enjoyed huge leads in the opinion polls, helped for once by a press campaign against the government even by papers which usually backed the Conservatives. In April 1964 the Labour party won control of the Greater London Council. Wilson challenged his opponents to dissolve parliament, berating them as having 'neither the guts to govern nor the grace to go'.

When eventually they went to the country the results were close, Labour obtaining 317 seats, the Conservatives 304 and the Liberals 9, giving Wilson, now prime minister, an overall majority of 4. The votes cast for the two major parties were even closer, 12,205,814 voting Labour, 12,001,396 voting Conservative. Labour's share of the poll was only marginally higher than it had been in 1959, up from 43.8 per cent to 44.1. The Liberals fared far better than both in many ways, seeing their vote rise to over 3 million and their share of those cast to 11.2 per cent. Despite this remarkable renaissance, however, they only gained nine seats in the Commons.

Both Labour and Liberal parties benefited from voters polling in a

WESTMINSTER
THEATRE
——
ENTIRELY
NEW
PRODUCTION
AND
CAST

13 YEARS
LONDON'S
LONGEST
RUN

VICKY

WHAT VARIOUS TRANSFORMATIONS WE REMARK,
FROM EAST WHITECHAPEL TO WEST HYDE PARK!
MEN, WOMEN, CHILDREN, HOUSES, SIGNS AND FASHIONS,
STATE, STAGE, TRADE, TASTE, THE HUMOURS AND THE PASSIONS;
THE EXCHANGE, 'CHANGE ALLEY, WHERESOE'ER YOU'RE RANGING,
COURT, CITY, COUNTRY, ALL ARE CHANGED OR CHANGING ...
··· AS CHANGE THUS CIRCULATES THROUGHOUT THE NATION,
SOME PLAYS MAY JUSTLY CALL FOR ALTERATIONS!

—FROM THE PROLOGUE OF 'A TRIP TO SCARBOROUGH'

34   Labour replaces the Conservatives in office: cartoon by
Vicky

parliamentary election for the first time. Indeed it has been calculated
that had the 1964 election been held on the 1959 register Labour would
not have won. Television also played a major part in this election for
the first time. This probably offset the partisanship of the press, which
reverted to form as the prospect of a campaign came closer.
Geographically the south of England apart from London, the midlands
and Wales did not swing towards Labour as much as the capital, the
north of England and above all Scotland. The Scottish results were
especially serious for the Conservatives, for their seats north of the
border slumped from thirty-one in 1959 to twenty-four. The Conservatives have not gained a majority of seats in Scotland since 1955, but the
1964 election marks the moment when they became a minority party
there, for they never improved on their performance then. The forty-
three Labour members returned from Scottish constituencies gave
Wilson a working majority.

   The hopes raised among his supporters at the polls were doomed to disappointment. So far from reversing the economic decline which Labour politicians had blamed on the Conservatives, they found themselves in the grip of apparently uncontrollable economic forces. They inherited a deficit on the balance of payments serious enough for them to try to redress by an immediate import surcharge of 15 per cent, and the negotiation of a loan of $1,000,000 from the International Monetary Fund. This only temporarily bailed out the current account on overseas trade. Although the import surcharge was reduced to 10 per cent in 1965, $1,400,000 was drawn from the IMF, and measures were taken to reduce consumer demand. The ultimate measure to redress the situation, however, the devaluation of the pound, was deliberately shunned. This was more on political than on economic grounds. So far from treasury orthodoxy dictating the avoidance of devaluing at all costs, officials there drew up contingent plans for what many considered to be inevitable. Wilson was all too aware, however, that Labour would be pilloried as the party of devaluation by the Conservatives and that this would probably be electorally damaging at a time when a general election might have to take place any day.

For the government's precarious parliamentary position became even more perilous when its designated foreign secretary, who had been defeated in 1964, also failed to win a by-election. The overall majority was reduced to three, and at least two Labour backbenchers were not ready to toe the party line on all issues, effectively vetoing, for instance, a bill to renationalise the steel industry.

Despite these difficulties, plans for expansion were made. A new department of economic affairs was created which, in consultation with the TUC and the newly formed Confederation of British Industries, published a national plan in 1965, which held out the prospect of an annual growth rate of 3.8 per cent. The solution to Britain's failure to match its rivals in productivity was sought in the agreement of both sides of industry to limit increases in prices and wages, in order to make British manufacturing more competitive. To monitor this policy a prices and incomes board was set up and a 'norm' of 3 per cent wage increases announced.

Wilson waited for the first sign that a general election would improve his party's position in the Commons. It came when a by-election held in Hull in January 1966 produced a swing to Labour which if repeated across the country would increase his majority.

Almost immediately after, the prime minister announced that parliament would be dissolved at the end of March.

The results vindicated Wilson's judgement. The number of Labour MPs went up from 316 on the eve of the polls to 363, and his majority from 2 to 96. Over 13 million people voted Labour for the first time since 1951, while the Conservative vote fell below 12 million for the first time since 1945. The Liberal vote also fell from over three million in 1964 to 2,327,533. Again, thanks to the vagaries of the electoral system, they won three more seats in 1966, raising their total to twelve.

Labour blamed its difficulties on the record of the previous Conservative administration, while the Conservatives attributed them to Labour's performance in office. The electorate gave the government the benefit of the doubt. Voters also preferred Wilson to the new Conservative leader Edward Heath, who had beaten his rivals for the leadership in the first poll for that position which was held when Sir Alec Douglas-Home resigned it in 1965. For the first time Labour had increased its majority, leading the prime minister to boast that it was the natural party of government.

Yet, though Wilson won the election, he could not win the battle to control the economy. Once again he was blown off course, this time by a strike of the National Union of Seamen which had devastating effects on Britain's trading account. This was followed by a run on the pound which threatened the devaluation he dreaded. Something of his feelings of helplessness to manage the economy at this time came out in his attribution of his troubles to conspirators; a 'tightly knit group of politically motivated men' in the case of the seamen's strike, 'the gnomes of Zurich' in that of the sterling speculators. He even began to suspect the BBC of partiality towards his political opponents. To stave off a devaluation of the pound, which many now regarded as inevitable, the government introduced the most drastic cuts on its spending programme coupled with draconian reductions in consumer demand. A compulsory prices and incomes policy was introduced. The cabinet even decided by a small majority that entry into the Common Market might after all help to solve Britain's balance of payments problems, despite Labour's opposition to the previous application in 1961. Like Macmillan before him, however, Wilson had to bear the humiliation of a veto from President de Gaulle of France in 1967.

The measures taken the previous July were not sufficient for sterling to withstand another bout of speculation, following a war between Israel and Egypt in the summer of 1967 which left the Suez Canal closed to shipping, and a record balance of payments deficit in October. On 18 November the pound was devalued from $2.80 to $2.40. The prime minister tried to put a fair face on it by claiming that 'The pound in your pocket has not been devalued' but this time his attempt to claim a triumph for a disaster was unconvincing.

The unpopularity of the government was recorded in a series of by-election defeats. The most sensational was the victory of a Scottish Nationalist in Hamilton, previously regarded as a safe Labour seat, in November 1967, which heralded a revival of nationalism in Scotland. Although this alarmed both major parties, with the Conservative leader announcing his support for a Scottish assembly in 1968, it stood to harm Labour more since it had more Scottish seats to lose. The Welsh Nationalist party, Plaid Cymru, also came close to winning apparently rock solid Labour constituencies in South Wales.

The electoral fortunes of the government seemed to improve as another severe squeeze on demand in the budget of 1968 began to exert a beneficial effect on the balance of payments, producing surpluses by the summer of 1969. Public opinion polls started to register a lead for the Labour party, suggesting that the government would win a general election, especially with the help of young voters between the ages of eighteen and twenty-one, who were expected to support the party which enfranchised them in 1968. The media proclaimed a third victory for Labour. Even the American magazine *Time* depicted the prime minister on its front cover, with the caption 'Will success spoil Harold Wilson?' The Cabinet decided to go to the polls in June 1970, confidently expecting a majority.

In the event, to the surprise of the pundits, the Conservatives emerged successful, with 330 seats to Labour's 288, while the Liberals obtained 6 seats and the Scottish Nationalists 1. This was an average swing of nearly 5 per cent, the largest to any party since 1945.

The pundits tried to redeem their credibility by claiming that there was a late swing to the Conservatives which one poll picked up. This they attributed to the publication of the May balance of payments figures, which revealed a monthly deficit on the eve of the polls. But, while there was increasing evidence for a volatile electorate, coupled with a tendency for the underlying state of the economy to be the most

35 Winifred Ewing with Arthur Donaldson at the Scottish National party's meeting at Bannockburn, 1971

crucial factor in parliamentary elections, such volatility based on one set of economic indicators seems too mechanical an explanation of the Conservative election victory in 1970. There were other causes for the Labour defeat besides the government's handling of the economy. Its dealings with challenges to its authority abroad and at home also affected its electoral standing. The outbreak of sectarian violence in Northern Ireland brought the problems of that province on to the agenda of British politics for the first time in forty years. In 1969 the army was sent to keep the peace between Catholics and Protestants. This soon proved to be a forlorn hope, for although troops were welcomed at first their presence came to be resented. While the army was thus employed a military solution to the situation posed by the unilateral declaration of independence by Rhodesia was ruled out, and instead sanctions were imposed. An attempt to deal with strikes by providing for a cooling-off period, and even the holding of ballots among union members, was bitterly resisted by the TUC, provoking a rebellion among Labour backbenchers and unease among ministers until the White Paper outlining the proposals, *In Place of Strife*, was dropped. Although an informal agreement was made between the government and the TUC to monitor strike action, the outcome was a blow for the ministry's prestige.

While none of these developments could be said to have brought about the downfall of the Wilson administration, together they contributed to an impression that it was being pushed around by forces (the IRA, the white Rhodesians, above all the British trade unions) over which it had no control. Some traditional Labour supporters apparently became disillusioned with the party, for the number of votes for it dropped by nearly 900,000 over the total cast in 1966, which was disproportionate to the lower turn-out at the second election. At the same time, many voters clearly thought that the fresh team of Edward Heath and his colleagues at the head of the Conservatives offered a better chance of solving problems which Wilson's cabinet, looking distinctly jaded after six years, had signally failed to solve. Certainly they did not look to the Liberals for solutions, for that party's vote fell slightly in 1970, while the Conservatives' picked up by 1,726,690 over 1966.

In the event, however, the Heath ministry failed to fulfil expectations. The situation in Northern Ireland deteriorated further, with the killing of the first British soldier in 1971, and of thirteen Catholics in Londonderry on 'Bloody Sunday' in 1972. Heath tried the experiments of direct rule from Westminster and power sharing in the province, but the first alienated the republican sympathisers among the Catholics, while the second provoked Protestant workers to go on strike in protest. Attempts to resolve the Rhodesian problem were also fruitless. As for standing up to challenges to the government's authority from the trades unions, Heath's record was even more dismal than Wilson's. Although he had no difficulty passing an Industrial Relations Act in 1971, enforcing it proved altogether different. So far from reducing the incidence of strikes their numbers increased dramatically, with a particularly challenging miners' strike in 1972, which resulted in an arbitrated settlement which gave the miners wage increases of between 17 and 24 per cent. Alarmed by wage awards of such magnitude, the government tried to effect a complete freeze on wages to be followed by statutory controls on increases. The more powerful trades unions, particularly the National Union of Mineworkers, were all set to challenge this policy when the government was overwhelmed by events totally outside its control, the Yom Kippur War of 1973 between the Arabs and the Israelis followed by a massive rise in world oil prices. The prime minister took the rare step of calling a state of emergency in November, and the following month declared a three-day week. Early in the new year the miners, their position immeasurably strengthened by the rise in oil prices, declared a national strike. Heath decided to call a general election on the issue of 'Who governs?' which gave rise to the myth that the miners brought down his government. In fact he chose to go to the country because he hoped that the issue would retain his position in the opinion polls, which began to show a lead for the Conservatives after a period in which they had trailed. In February 1974 therefore the country went to the polls.

The outcome of the election of February 1974 was a 'hung' parliament. In the highest turn-out since the 1950s the voters returned to Westminster 301 Labour MPs, 297 Conservatives, 14 Liberals, and 9 Scottish and Welsh Nationalists. Heath tried to cling to power by doing a deal with the Liberal leader Jeremy Thorpe, but negotiations broke down when the prime minister refused to concede proportional representation, even though his own party had obtained a slightly higher proportion of the votes cast than had Labour. That the Liberals should have made this the condition of joining any coalition could scarcely have surprised him, since they polled nearly a fifth of the votes but obtained only fourteen seats, 2 per cent of the total.

Having failed to form a government Heath surrendered office to Harold Wilson. It was clear that the incoming Labour ministry would call another general election as soon as the possibility of obtaining an overall majority presented itself. Over the summer the opinion polls

36 Edward Heath, seated between Sir Alec Douglas-Home and Geoffrey Rippon, signing Britain's agreement to enter the EEC in 1972

indicated that an autumn election would produce a Labour landslide. Wilson consequently dissolved parliament in October, but as in 1970 was misled by the pundits. So far from obtaining a comfortable margin over all other parties he scarcely obtained a working majority, Labour emerging from the polls with an overall lead of three seats. Turn-out fell between February and October from 78.1 per cent to 72.8. The Conservatives suffered most from this, losing over a million votes. The Liberals lost over 700,000 votes and one of their fourteen seats.

Perhaps the main casualty of the outcome of the election was Mr Heath himself. In 1975 the Conservatives passed judgement on his poor electoral performance by replacing him as leader with Margaret Thatcher. Though his record as prime minister had not endeared him to the party faithful, he had one triumph to his name which in the long run was to eclipse any failures attributed to his premiership, transforming him in later years into an elder statesman. This was his successful negotiation of Britain's entry into the European Economic Community. At the time of his electoral victory in 1970 the EEC invited his government to apply. Parliament endorsed the decision to join in principle by 356 votes to 244 in October 1971. The following January

37   Labour's decision to resolve its disagreements over Europe
by a referendum, as satirised in the *Sunday Telegraph*, 26 January
1975

the treaty of accession was signed, and in October 1972 the European
Communities Act became law. Britain formally entered the 'Common
Market' on 1 January 1973. The Labour party was deeply divided on
this issue, and Wilson endeavoured to hold it together by going
through the motions of renegotiating the terms, and then putting the
matter to the consideration of the electorate in a unique referendum.
On 5 June 1975 voters were asked to reply 'yes' or 'no' to the question
'Do you think that the United Kingdom should stay in the European
Community (Common Market)?' Some 28,954,443, or 64.3 per cent of
those registered, responded in Britain (compared with under half the
electorate in Northern Ireland). Of these 66.7 per cent voted 'yes' in
England and Wales, while the Scots were less enthusiastic, 58.4 being
in favour in Scotland. Indeed the only counties where a majority voted
'no' were Shetland and the Western Isles. Nationally there could be no
doubt that membership of the European Community had substantial
support. The referendum put paid to speculation about the attitude of
Britons to the Common Market and also, incidentally, not so much to
'a thousand years of history' as to 268, the epoch between the Anglo-
Scottish Union of 1707 over which, perhaps fortunately, no referendum
was held, and Britain's entry into Europe.

Epilogue

Just as there were optimists and pessimists at the time of the Anglo-Scottish Union about the economic prospects facing Scotland as it was swallowed up in the larger entity of the new United Kingdom, so there were prophets of a miracle and predicters of disaster about the fate of Great Britain in the European Community, or Common Market as it was commonly called. On both occasions the Cassandras could have the cold comfort of saying 'we told you so', for there was no immediate boost to the Scottish economy following the Union, or to the British economy after entry into Europe. Indeed there were Scots after 1707, and Britons after 1973, who argued that their absorption into a wider community had been disastrous, and that it would be better to retreat from the commitment, reasserting Scottish or British independence. All that the advocates of surrendering sovereignty could urge, on both occasions, was that the alternatives would be even worse.

In the short run the benefits of the Union were perhaps outweighed by the disadvantages. But, until the late twentieth century at least, in the long run most Scots came to accept that they were better off as North Britons than they would have been had they remained independent. It is too early yet for Britons to make the same assessment of their involvement with Europe. The issues it provokes are too emotive and pressing for a dispassionate appraisal to be made. A historical verdict cannot be predicted, but it is tempting to conjecture that the outcome of the current debate over membership of the EC will be resolved in much the same way as the dispute over the Anglo-Scottish Union.

MONARCHS AND MINISTRIES

1707–1976

1707–1714	Queen Anne	1707–1710	Lord Godolphin
		1710–1714	Robert Harley, Earl of Oxford
1714–1727	King George I	1714–1721	Lords Stanhope and Sunderland
		1721–1727	Lord Townsend and Sir Robert Walpole
1727–1760	King George II	1727–1742	Sir Robert Walpole
		1742–1743	Lord Carteret and Earl of Wilmington
		1743–1754	Henry Pelham and Duke of Newcastle
		1754–1756	Duke of Newcastle
		1756–1757	William Pitt and Duke of Devonshire
		1757–1760	William Pitt and Duke of Newcastle
1760–1820	King George III	1760–1762	William Pitt and Duke of Newcastle
		1762–1763	Earl of Bute
		1763–1765	George Grenville
		1765–1766	Marquis of Rockingham
		1766–1768	Earl of Chatham
		1768–1770	Duke of Grafton
		1770–1782	Lord North
		1782	Marquis of Rockingham
		1782–1783	Earl of Shelburne

		1783	Charles James Fox and Lord North
		1783–1801	William Pitt the Younger
		1801–1804	Henry Addington
		1804–1806	William Pitt
		1806–1807	Lord Grenville
		1807–1809	Duke of Portland
		1809–1812	Spencer Perceval
		1812–1820	Earl of Liverpool
1820–1830	King George IV	1820–1827	Earl of Liverpool
		1827	George Canning
		1827–1828	Viscount Goderich
		1828–1830	Duke of Wellington
1830–1837	King William IV	1830–1834	Earl Grey
		1834	Viscount Melbourne
		1834	Duke of Wellington
		1834–1835	Sir Robert Peel
		1835–1837	Viscount Melbourne
1837–1901	Queen Victoria	1837–1841	Viscount Melbourne
		1841–1846	Sir Robert Peel
		1846–1852	Lord John Russell
		1852	Earl of Derby
		1852–1855	Earl of Aberdeen
		1855–1858	Viscount Palmerston
		1858–1859	Earl of Derby
		1859–1865	Viscount Palmerston
		1865–1866	Earl Russell
		1866–1868	Earl of Derby
		1868	Benjamin Disraeli
		1868–1873	William Ewart Gladstone
		1874–1880	Benjamin Disraeli
		1880–1885	William Ewart Gladstone
		1885–1886	Marquis of Salisbury
		1886	William Ewart Gladstone
		1886–1892	Marquis of Salisbury
		1892–1894	William Ewart Gladstone
		1894–1895	Earl of Rosebery
		1895–1901	Marquis of Salisbury
1901–1910	King Edward VII	1901–1902	Marquis of Salisbury
		1902–1905	Arthur James Balfour
		1905–1908	Sir Henry Campbell-Bannerman
		1908–1910	Herbert Henry Asquith

1910–1936	King George V	1910–1916	Herbert Henry Asquith
		1916–1922	David Lloyd George
		1922–1923	Andrew Bonar Law
		1923–1924	Stanley Baldwin
		1924	James Ramsey MacDonald
		1924–1929	Stanley Baldwin
		1929–1931	James Ramsay MacDonald
		1931–1935	James Ramsay MacDonald
		1935–1936	Stanley Baldwin
1936	King Edward VIII	1936	Stanley Baldwin
1936–1952	King George VI	1936–1937	Stanley Baldwin
		1937–1940	Neville Chamberlain
		1940–1945	Winston Churchill
		1945–1951	Clement Attlee
		1951–1952	Sir Winston Churchill
1952	Queen Elizabeth II	1952–1955	Sir Winston Churchill
		1955–1957	Sir Anthony Eden
		1957–1963	Harold Macmillan
		1963–1964	Sir Alec Douglas-Home
		1964–1970	Harold Wilson
		1970–1974	Edward Heath
		1974–1976	Harold Wilson

GUIDE TO FURTHER READING

Among the many one-volume overviews of modern British history Glyn Williams and John Ramsden, *Ruling Britannia: A Political History of Britain 1688–1988* (Longman, 1990), which contains a full and up-to-date bibliography, is outstanding. Longman have also produced a series, 'Foundations of Modern Britain', under the general editorship of Geoffrey Holmes. Two volumes have appeared which deal with the period covered by this book: Eric J. Evans, *The Forging of the Modern State: Early Industrial Britain 1783–1870* (1983); and Keith Robbins, *The Eclipse of a Great Power: Modern Britain 1870–1975* (1983). Geoffrey Holmes's own volumes for the years 1660–1783 are eagerly awaited. Meanwhile the new Oxford History of England has made its debut with Paul Langford's *A Polite and Commercial People: England 1727–1783* (1989). When all the volumes have appeared they will render the former series entirely obsolete, with the exception of A. J. P. Taylor's classic *English History 1914–1945* (1965), available in a Pelican paperback (1970). Oxford University Press have also published two relevant titles in their 'Shorter Oxford History' series: Norman McCord, *British History 1815–1906* (1991); and T. O. Lloyd, *Empire to Welfare State: English History 1906–1985* (3rd edition, 1989).

INDEX